General editor: Graham Handley MA

Brodie's Notes on Charles Dickens s
Oliver Twist

Graham Handley MA PhD
Formerly Principal Lecturer and Head of English Department, The College of All Saints, Tottenham

Pan Books London and Sydney

This revised edition published 1986 by Pan Books Ltd
Cavaye Place, London SW10 9PG
9 8 7 6 5 4 3 2 1
© Graham Handley 1986
ISBN 0 330 50228 X
Photoset by Parker Typesetting Service, Leicester
Printed and bound in Great Britain by
Richard Clay (The Chaucer Press) Ltd, Bungay, Suffolk

This book is sold subject to the condition that it
shall not, by way of trade or otherwise, be lent, re-sold,
hired out or otherwise circulated without the publisher's prior
consent in any form of binding or cover other than that in which
it is published and without a similar condition including this
condition being imposed on the subsequent purchaser

Contents

Preface by the general editor   5

The author and his work   7

Literary terms used in these notes   10

Background and setting   11

Plot and structure   13

Chapter summaries, critical commentaries, textual notes and revision questions   17

Dickens's art in *Oliver Twist*   74

The characters
Oliver 75, Rose Maylie 77, Harry Maylie 78, Fagin and Sikes 78, Bumble and Mrs Bumble 79, Noah Claypole and Charlotte 80, Monks 81, The Dodger 81, Nancy 82, Minor characters 83

Style   87

General questions   93

Further reading   96

Page references in these Notes are to the Penguin Classics edition of *Oliver Twist*, but references are also given to particular chapters, so that the Notes may be used with any edition of the novel.

Preface

The intention throughout this study aid is to stimulate and guide, to encourage the reader's *involvement* in the text, to develop disciplined critical responses and a sure understanding of the main details in the chosen text.

Brodie's Notes provide a summary of the plot of the play or novel followed by act, scene or chapter summaries, each of which will have an accompanying critical commentary designed to underline the most important literary and factual details. Textual notes will be explanatory or critical (sometimes both), defining what is difficult or obscure on the one hand, or stressing points of character, style or plot on the other. Revision questions will be set on each act or group of chapters to test the student's careful application to the text of the prescribed book.

The second section of each of these study aids will consist of a critical examination of the author's art. This will cover such major elements as characterization, style, structure, setting, theme(s) or any other aspect of the book which the editor considers needs close study. The paramount aim is to send the student back to the text. Each study aid will include a series of general questions which require a detailed knowledge of the set book; the first of these questions will have notes by the editor of what *might* be included in a written answer. A short list of books considered useful as background reading for the student will be provided at the end.

Graham Handley

The author and his work

The biographies and critical studies of Charles Dickens – and they show no signs of abating – are testimony to the powerful hold he has exerted on the reading public ever since the first appearance of *Sketches by Boz* (1833–4). In the eyes of many he stands next to Shakespeare; television plays and scripts are written about his life or aspects of it, and his books are filmed, adapted, or turned into musicals (Lionel Bart's *Oliver!*, for example), with flattering regularity and ingenuity. The biography, *Charles Dickens*, by his friend and adviser John Forster, tantalizes both by what it reveals and what it omits; while F. R. Leavis, perhaps the most influential critic of the novel in the twentieth century, has recanted his view (expressed in *The Great Tradition*, 1948) that Dickens was merely 'a great entertainer'.

This study aid can do no more than give the outlines of a crowded life, both creative and social, direct the student to the experience of a great writer, and perhaps to some of the critical and biographical works which will help to extend his own experience of the books. Childhood exercised a peculiar influence on Dickens, perhaps because he felt that his own was scarred, and the student of *Oliver Twist* should read those other novels which explore the trials and tribulations of childhood: *David Copperfield, Hard Times* and *Great Expectations*.

Born in 1812 in Portsmouth, the second eldest son in a family of eight, Dickens saw his improvident father and the rest of the family incarcerated for debt in the Marshalsea Debtors' Prison. This experience was to receive full treatment in *Little Dorrit* (1855–7): Charles spent six weeks working in Warren's blacking warehouse before his father's release and his own despatch to school. Again he was haunted by what he had endured, and part of the autobiographical element of *David Copperfield* records the anguish of the time. Dickens lived as he wrote, with zest and with an unrivalled capacity for experiencing both the ecstasy and the melancholy and later incorporating these extremes into his fiction. He worked in an attorney's office; then as a reporter in Doctors' Commons, teaching himself shorthand and quickly striking out as a writer himself under the pseudonym of 'Boz'.

The first sketches referred to above were followed by the episodic *Pickwick Papers* (1836–7), which were originally commissioned as a vehicle for the artist Seymour; their verve and humour, their presentation of a range of eccentric and idiosyncratic characters, and the animated and ebullient style and control of situation, established the young author who, before he had finished them, became editor of *Bentley's Miscellany*, and began to write *Oliver Twist*, the first number appearing in the magazine in February 1837.

In May 1837 his sister-in-law Mary Hogarth died; she had lived with her sister and Charles since their marriage, and Dickens adored her. She died in his arms; he took a ring from her finger, and wore it until his own death. He dreamed of her continually, and there is little doubt that many of the heroines of his fiction are derived from the purity and perfection he found in her.

Oliver Twist was followed by *Nicholas Nickleby* (1838–9), an attack on the Yorkshire farm schools. Dickens was never less than prolific, and *The Old Curiosity Shop* (1840), *Barnaby Rudge* (1841) and *Martin Chuzzlewit* (1843–4) indicate his capacity for giving himself wholeheartedly to the career he had already made so successful to himself. Active socially, theatrically, politically, philanthropically (his letters reveal the amazing range of his interests and concerns), he spent longer from now on than hitherto between his novels. But increasingly a growing sense of artistic structure came upon him, and from *Dombey and Son* (1846–8) that awareness is present in the complex handling of plot and sub-plot, of contrast and parallel, of image and symbol. Of course it leads to the creation of the long and bulky novel (which Henry James referred to as 'loose, baggy monsters'), and these perhaps deter the modern reader from total immersion in Dickens. They occupy the middle section of Dickens's career, with *David Copperfield* (1848–50), perhaps the best-loved, and *Bleak House* (1852–3), the most aesthetically pleasing. Between that and the prison-riddled *Little Dorrit* (1855–7), Dickens sandwiched a small masterpiece, *Hard Times* (1854), set in the (for him) distant provincial location of Preston (Coketown). He had spent much of his time in Paris, and a reading of Carlyle's *French Revolution* is said to have kindled a desire to write *A Tale of Two Cities* (1859), with its graphic reconstruction of events great and small in that turbulent era. But strictly speaking the last period of Dickens's writing begins with *Great Expectations* (1860–61), thought by some critics to be the high watermark of his achievement. It is rich in the experiences of childhood and in atmosphere and, as in *Our Mutual Friend* (1864–5), there is no evidence of any falling off, either in the verve or the vivacity of the writing or of the imagination that informed it. The final work, *Edwin Drood* (1870), which seemed to be breaking new ground, was left incomplete by the author's death. Then there were his stories (remember, for example, that ever-popular allegory, *A Christmas Carol*, 1843), the playlets, essays and speeches.

No mention has been made here of Dickens's private life, save the reference to Mary Hogarth's death, and his devotion to her. A description of the separation from his wife and his relationship with Ellen Ternan is, we feel, irrelevant to these study notes. Like most writers, Dickens is surrounded by anecdote and gossip, by interpretations of the sensational and investigations of the peripheral. The student of *Oliver Twist* – or of any of the novels or stories for that matter – should first concentrate on the particular work in question; then he or she can turn to this study aid for critical explanations and commentaries.

Dickens was – and perhaps is, despite our turning away to media other than print – a national institution, the great fireside communicator of his own time and well into this century. But for many of us the fireside has gone, and the voices that speak to us are not rich in humanity or in social, moral or spiritual concern. Dickens is all these, and that is perhaps why we should read him so attentively today. For as we see Oliver ask for more; Dombey awaken to love for his daughter after the years of silent rejection; Pip's discovery of himself in his affection for Magwitch; or Lizzie Hexam's insistent sacrifice for her brother Charley's education, we touch the immutable fibres of human love beside which the computers and screens of our own time are ephemeral and irrelevant.

Literary terms used in these Notes

The section on *Style* (pp.87–92) sufficiently defines Dickens's main usages, but a short list is included below.

Metaphor The use of a comparison without employing the words *like* or *as*.
Simile The use of a comparison introduced by the words *like* or *as*.
Irony There are various forms, the main one being the opposite meaning of what is being said, i.e. the 'merry old gentleman', descriptive of Fagin, who is in reality a dark and unscrupulous criminal.
Malapropism Derived from Mrs Malaprop in Sheridan's play *The Rivals* (1775). She confused similar-sounding words just as the Artful Dodger does in such a phrase as 'Did you redress [address] yourself to me, my man?'

Background and setting

This is both geographical and historical. Oliver begins life in a workhouse some distance from London – seventy-five miles, as becomes clear in Chapter 8 – and on the seventh morning of his flight he limps 'into the little town of Barnet'. There he meets the Artful Dodger, who objects to being in London in daylight; they enter by 'the turnpike at Islington' at nearly eleven o'clock. Then follows an exact description of the remainder of the journey:

> They crossed from the Angel in St John's Road; struck down the small street which terminates at Sadler's Wells Theatre; through Exmouth Street and Coppice Row; down the little court by the side of the workhouse; across the classic ground which once bore the name of Hockley-in-the-Hole; thence into Little Saffron Hill; and so into Saffron Hill the Great . . . pushed open the door of a house near Field Lane; (p.102).

Certainly part of this route can still be traced merely by looking at Bartholomew's *Reference Atlas of Greater London*. We have, therefore, a reasonably accurate identification of Fagin's den; Field Lane was one of the most disgusting of the London slums and was demolished in the 1860s when Holborn Viaduct was built. The London setting is encompassed with exactitude, and later in the novel we could trace the journey of Sikes and Oliver to Chertsey; and again a look at the above-mentioned *Reference Atlas* would identify not only Chertsey but some of the places mentioned – for example, Lower Halliford and Shepperton. Even Sikes's despairing journey to escape the eyes and his conscience takes us only into Hertfordshire, to St Albans and Hatfield. The whole action of *Oliver Twist* is rooted in reality, and the identification of Mr Fang helps to give actuality, authenticity to the fictional narrative; he was based on Allan Stewart Laing, a Metropolitan magistrate who dispensed his injustice from Hatton Garden Police Court. When we find Mr Fang reading a newspaper we are aware that his mood is somewhat conditioned by the nature of the reports – against himself – that he is reading. In fact Laing was afterwards removed from the court for his malpractice. It will be seen from this that the geographical setting is fairly easy to establish, while Mr Fang represents Dickens's authentic documentation of an aspect of his fiction.

The passing historical reference above to Fang's progenitor, Laing (Dickens was smuggled into court to see him in action), is set against a much broader issue, which indeed forms the substance of the early part of the novel: the Poor Law Amendment Act of 1834. Mrs Mann's, where Oliver originally stays, is an old-style baby farm, but when he is carried back to the workhouse by Bumble the effects of the new Poor Law are being felt, and we see why it is that Dickens attacked the 'philosophers' responsible for it. Under the old system the numbers of unemployed had grown, and this meant that many men capable of work found themselves on parish relief and chose to stay on it. The amendment sought to get these men working, and to discourage childbearing among paupers by reducing the diets in the workhouses and segregating the sexes. The ideal behind it was not as offensive as the practice, which Dickens so bitterly attacks in his accounts of the gruel served, and the desperation of Oliver and his companions that ultimately leads to his asking for more. Moreover, those responsible for the Poor Law Amendment Act did not take into account local conditions, want of money, corruption at beadle and workhouse matron and overseer level, all of which Dickens exposes through character in *Oliver Twist*. Cruelty of any kind to children touched Dickens himself so closely that his impassioned moral indignation was the result. Dickens is the great exposer of social evil, and you may feel as you read the novel that the real criminals are Mr Bumble, Mrs Corney, Mrs Mann and the gentleman in the white waistcoat, as well as Sowerberry and Gamfield, who are both ready to 'buy' a pauper and use him for their own ends. Yet the named criminals are Fagin, Sikes and the Dodger, and to the reader who wishes to know more of this area of Dickens's work, Philip Collins's masterly study, *Dickens and Crime*, is strongly recommended. Even the presentation of Nancy is characterized, one feels, by Dickens's wish to reclaim the prostitutes he saw so often in his night-walks through London. Thus in *Oliver Twist* we are given 'a local habitation and a name', for the areas are real, and many of them have survived to this day. But the reality that existed in their time – the maladministration of the Poor Law and the prevalence of widespread organized crime as a social evil – these are the stuff of *Oliver Twist*.

Plot and structure

Before looking closely at the plot and the structure of *Oliver Twist*, the interested student who wishes to work at some depth should study the definitive edition edited by Kathleen Tillotson (The Clarendon Edition, Oxford University Press, pp.369–71). There he will find listed the chapters of the novel as they appeared each month in *Bentley's Miscellany*, and will be able to judge from this how Dickens aimed to secure the interest of his readers over a long period of publication. He may be able to account for switches in the narrative, for movements from one part of the plot into another, for scenes of comedy alternating with scenes of strong social comment or criminal action. In mid-career Dickens became progressively more aware of structure, but there is every evidence to support the view that *Oliver Twist* is carefully constructed, particularly in terms of parallel and contrast; and wherever possible this is indicated in the notes to the chapters.

The plot of the novel is complex in the working out and in the rather elaborate laying of clues (witness the portrait of Agnes Fleming in Brownlow's room where Oliver is lying ill), but in outline – and with the hindsight of having read the novel – we can see that it is relatively simple. Oliver Twist is born in a workhouse and subjected to abuse and ill-treatment both there and at the child farm run by Mrs Mann; with the connivance of the authorities he is apprenticed to Mr Sowerberry (because of a kindly magistrate, they have failed to hand him over body and soul to Mr Gamfield), but having been beaten by his employer Oliver runs away. Befriended by the Artful Dodger, he goes to London and falls under the control of Fagin, who by the simple expedient of playing games tries to turn him into a pickpocket.

When he first goes out with Charley Bates and the Dodger, Oliver is mistakenly thought to have committed the theft expertly achieved by the Dodger, and is arrested and taken before the brutal magistrate Mr Fang. He is released on the evidence of the bookstall owner, and is taken back to Mr Brownlow's house, where he recovers; meanwhile, Fagin, incensed by Oliver's escape, sends Nancy out to the police office to find him. Eventually they kidnap Oliver when he goes out to return some books for Mr Brownlow and, after keeping him for some time, send him out with Sikes and Toby Crackit to burgle the Maylies' house at Chertsey. It is at this stage that we have to break off from the straight sequence of the narrative and take into account what is revealed later – the plotting of Monks to keep Oliver in a life of corruption. Monks's real name is Edward Leeford and his father, while living apart from his mother, fell in love with Agnes Fleming who had a child by him – Oliver. Edward's father dies, leaving the bulk of his property to Agnes and her unborn child, rather than to his wife and son, Edward. They destroy the will but, thinking that the boy may appear later, Edward searches for him, finds that he has left the workhouse where he was born, discovers him in Fagin's den and enters into a deal with Fagin to keep the boy corrupted.

This brings us back to the Maylie burglary and the reason for Fagin's dismay when he learns that Sikes has left Oliver behind. Fagin and Monks lay a plot to kidnap Oliver yet again (Oliver does see them by the window at the Maylie house) but this scheme is foiled by Nancy who, seeing in Oliver innocence unsullied by crime, reveals what she knows to Rose Maylie. Nancy's watching over Oliver leads her to tell Rose and Mr Brownlow of Monks's wickedness and of the implication of Fagin, and this, overheard by the newly recruited Noah Claypole and retailed to Sikes at Fagin's instigation, leads to Nancy's murder at the hands of the man she loves.

Sikes flees from justice, Mr Brownlow identifies Monks and interrogates him, forcing him to reveal the secret of Oliver's birth and inheritance, and first Fagin is arrested, then Sikes inadvertently kills himself in trying to escape from the mob. Fagin is hanged, Monks dies abroad in a prison, and it is revealed that Rose Maylie is really Rose Fleming, the sister of Oliver's mother and thus his aunt. Fagin's gang disintegrates, Charley Bates becomes a grazier, Mr Brownlow adopts Oliver, Rose marries Harry Maylie, and Mr and Mrs Bumble end their days as paupers in the workhouse they once ruled.

This is the outline of the book, and the student who is confused by the direction of the narrative should refer to it constantly. The *structure* is sufficient indication of Dickens's early craftsmanship. The sequence of the novel can be divided as follows:

Chapters 1–7 Strictly speaking, the workhouse and related sequence, from the birth of Oliver, through his maltreatment, his apprenticeship to Sowerberry, his determination to leave after the clash with Noah Claypole and his subsequent thrashing at the hands of the undertaker.

Chapters 8–11 Oliver meeting the Dodger, Fagin's den, Oliver arrested for pick-pocketing and taken before Mr Fang.

Chapters 12–15 Much use of contrast between Oliver in the Brownlow home on the one hand, and the plans of Fagin to kidnap him via Nancy on the other.

Chapters 16–22 Oliver re-taken and employed in the burglary at Chertsey.

Chapters 23–27 Fine alternation of the comedy courtship of Bumble and Mrs Corney, Fagin's reaction to the news of the failure of the burglary, the introduction of Monks, the revelation of old Sally – and a close look at this will show the *linking* (Bumbles, Fagin, Monks) which leads to the final unravelling of the plots and the hangman's noose.

Chapters 28–36 The lyrical interlude with but two disruptions – the illness of Rose and the appearance of Monks and Fagin, and the expert handling of Blathers and Duff by Losberne.

Chapters 37–41 The balance of contrasts – Bumble and his wife (she rules), Fagin and Monks, Nancy and Rose, and daylight morality showing in Nancy's decision to save Oliver.

Chapters 42–47 Again the contrast – the fall of the Dodger, the rise of Noah Claypole, Nancy and her betrayal of Monks and her supposed betrayal of Sikes, leading to the climax of her murder, and the beginning of the end for the criminals.

Chapters 48–52 The flight of Sikes, his part-expiation and his return to his death, the last night and death of Fagin, the winding up of all the plots.

It will be seen from the foregoing that there is a fine flow of narrative tension throughout; that Dickens's sense of structure at this stage means the alternation of action that is either graphic or comic, criminal or sentimentally lyrical; that he works through parallel and contrast in situation and character; and that the opposition is between good and evil, the sentimental and the sordid. In part, *structure* and *style* are linked, as we shall see when we consider the various modes of expression Dickens employs. The *appearance/reality* theme (e.g. Oliver's appearance as a criminal and the reality of his innocence) is very much part of the structure as well as the style of the novel.

We should note, too, that the *comedy* of *Oliver Twist* is part of its sombre structure: the games in Fagin's den (training in criminal expertise); and the courtship of Bumble and Mrs Corney (two can corrupt as effectively as one). This means that the *themes* of *Oliver Twist* – the attacks on the Poor Law system; on brutal magistrates; on incompetent Bow Street runners; on inhumanity and hypocrisy wherever they are practised under the guise of respectability; on the incidence of criminality and corruption and the deliberate spread of corruption – all these are part of the structural coherence of the book, and are seen both in relation to one another and in the perspective of real life.

Chapter summaries, critical commentaries, textual notes and revision questions

Chapter 1

Oliver is born in the workhouse, with the contracted doctor and the drunken old woman in attendance. His struggles for survival are finally successful. Meanwhile his mother, who wishes to die, succeeds, and the surgeon departs. Oliver is wrapped in a green blanket, cries, and the old woman returns to her bottle.

Commentary

The birth in the workhouse is immediately and effectively contrasted with the birth in family life, the emphasis being on the sordid nature of the surroundings and the drunken attendant. There is, too, immediate pathos in the dying mother's wish for death. Drama attends her identity, while the author's voice is employed in ironic contemplation of Oliver's prospects, being born in circumstances which ensure that his future will be a hard one. Already the social and moral commentary is evident, with the surgeon displaying some humanity but perhaps rather 'fancying' the good-looking girl who has no wedding ring to make the birth respectable.

the item of mortality The first of Dickens's ironic descriptions – the human being here seen as a statistic.
Although I am not disposed to maintain The author's use of his *own* voice is a commonplace of 19th-century fiction, having its origin in the practice of 18th-century novelists like Fielding. Dickens uses the convention to be ironic, rhetorical, to make witty or sarcastic asides, to be historical, philosophical and, most of all, to moralize. This first chapter is largely ironical at the expense of the workhouse system and its inhumanity and inefficiency.
he would most inevitably . . . have been killed in no time This time the irony is directed against the incompetence of the medical profession.
rather misty i.e. somewhat stupefied.
wurkus Workhouse.
consolatory perspective i.e. a high-flown way of saying 'soothing attitude'. The tone is still ironic.

They talked of hope and comfort. They had been strangers too long Notice the superb, antithetical combination of the impersonality of death and the personification of the qualities which would have made life worth living.

'Mrs Thingummy' Again the impersonality – the old woman is too low in status to have a name.

overseer's order i.e. by order of the parish officer charged with poor relief and other related offices.

the green bottle i.e. containing spirits, usually gin.

badged and ticketed i.e. given the symbol, the label, of what he was.

despised by all, and pitied by none Dickens is very fond of using economical antithesis – here finely direct in its implication.

Chapter 2

Oliver is 'brought up by hand'. He is farmed out to a branch workhouse where the old woman keeps the orphans on short supplies, appropriating to herself most of the allowance she gets for the orphans. The beadle always prepares the way for visits to the farm by going there the day before, to ensure that the paupers are cleaned up and ready to be inspected. Oliver is now aged nine and Mr Bumble, the beadle, visits Mrs Mann, 'the good lady of the house'. Bumble is a self-important character, but condescends to take a little gin with Mrs Mann. He has come to enquire about Oliver Twist, whose name he invented; then to return him to the main workhouse. Oliver pretends not to want to leave Mrs Mann, and does in fact cry when he goes. Arrived at the workhouse, Oliver appears before the Board. He is interrogated by the gentleman with the white waistcoat. He is told that he will pick oakum the next day; and that night he sobs himself to sleep. The Board's practices are then defined – the gradual starvation of the paupers by cutting rations has been implemented. This is followed by a description of the stone hall where they eat, the poverty of their diet, and the threat of one boy to eat another – which ultimately leads to the drawing of lots and Oliver's asking for more. This leads to his reappearance before the Board, and the decision of that charitable body to offer five pounds to anyone who will take him off their hands.

Commentary

This chapter involves the uncompromising exposure of the system. Its maladministration is directly attacked through its statistics, the author is ironic at the expense of the 'experimental philosopher', and the means of punishment are castigated. Self-important, pompous and inhumane, are words definitive of Mr Bumble, while the hypocrisy and subservience necessary for survival are shown in Mrs Mann. The exchanges between the two of them have a genuine comic flavour. This gives way to Oliver's loneliness when he leaves, fine pathos in view of the fact that Mrs Mann's farm has never been a home to him, yet it is the only home he has known.

The interview with the Board shows Dickens at his best, with its studied emphasis on man's inhumanity to man or here, more directly, man's inhumanity to child. The lack of Christianity and the lack of logic in the attitude of the Board are both stressed. Dickens waxes rhetorical, citing the 'tender laws of England' which allow paupers to sleep. The celebrated scene in which Oliver asks for more, moving though it is, has Dickens perhaps going over the top in his description of the master's response. Indolent and ignorant reaction is shown in the white-coated gentleman's assertion that Oliver will be hanged; the Board's and the workhouse's moral obloquy is obvious.

brought up by hand A favourite Dickensian phrase, much used in *Great Expectations* to explain Pip's ordeal at the hands of Mrs Joe in childhood; 'by hand' carries the terrible irony of being beaten, instead of the intimate care which it should imply.
Everybody knows the story This is another facet of the style in *Oliver Twist* – the narration of an instance or anecdote related to the main action (again the 18th-century precursor is Fielding). Here the anecdote deals with starvation.
gathered to the fathers it had never known Throughout Dickens's work there runs a loose vein of Christianity, a belief in Heaven and its justice.
remonstrance In this case, a petition of complaint.
the beadle Parish officer. The word has become associated with officialdom and thence by extension with 'officiousness'.
(which was very probable indeed) Dickens's ironic device – the use of the parenthesis or bracket for an aside.
this system of farming . . . luxuriant crop This time there is the running-on of the comparison, much used later in the novel with the sea and tide images that describe the crowd's pursuit of Sikes.
apparition Ghostly appearance.
(Susan, take Oliver . . . and wash 'em directly) Another good example of parenthetical usage – here revealing the reality beneath the appearance.

a parochial delegate and a stipendiary A pompous and high-flown way of saying that Mrs Mann is employed by the Parish.
He had displayed the one, and vindicated the other Another example of Dickens's use of antithesis.
beadles are but men . . . Heavy irony. Later we learn that Bumble is *not* a man in terms of courage.
Daffy A medicine for children, sometimes with added gin.
inflaming her left eye with the corner of her apron i.e. deliberately making it appear that she is moved or crying. Mrs Mann is up to all the tricks.
eight or ten fat gentlemen . . . a particularly fat gentleman In *Oliver Twist* Dickens makes a considered use of contrast, here to emphasize the comfortable well-fed nature of the Board as distinct from the half-starved state of the paupers for whom they are responsible.
others of the same race Read on, and you will see that the gentleman in the white waistcoat is himself a fool.
oakum Picking old rope to pieces for use in caulking (stopping up seams of ships).
elysium From the Greek, meaning a place, state, of ideal happiness.
Doctors' Commons The reference is to courts of civil law and their expense.
long-headed men i.e. wise, shrewd.
taking in the clothes i.e. making them smaller (because of the wasted nature of the children).
inmates got thin i.e. many died.
ecstasies i.e. (the Board) were very happy.
porringer Small basin from which soup is eaten.
per diem Daily.
short commons i.e. meagre meal.
As I purpose to show in the sequel We are never allowed to forget the author and his use of his own voice exercising control and directing our moral judgements.

Chapter 3

Here we find Oliver in solitary confinement – he hasn't even got the pocket-handkerchief with which to hang himself and thus fulfil the prediction of the gentleman in the white waistcoat. He washes in the yard under the pump, with some assistance from Bumble's cane; then he is publicly flogged each day as a warning to the other inmates, to whom he is held up as an agent of the Devil. Meanwhile, Mr Gamfield sees the notice about Oliver's availability on the workhouse gates. Having beaten his donkey, he outlines for the Board the humane way in which he treats the boys who sweep chimneys for him. The Board initially rejects his application, but then settles on a premium of three pounds, fifteen shillings for 'apprenticing' him. Oliver, given extra bread by Bumble, thinks that he is being fattened up to be killed. But when they go to the magistrate the latter, by sheer chance, sees Oliver's terrified countenance, and refuses to sign the indentures. He urges that Oliver be treated kindly.

Commentary

Heavy irony through the reference to 'the wisdom and mercy of the board' is followed by description of the stark nature of Oliver's existence. The sordidness and inhumanity of the financial bickering with Gamfield is stressed, the active collusion and unscrupulousness of the Board carrying its own moral indictment. As always, pathos attends the solitariness of Oliver, but the magistrate symbolizes the essential goodness of human nature in refusing to sign the indentures. There is effective contrast here between Bumble, Gamfield and the magistrate.

imprecation ... eyes Probably 'Damn your eyes'.
register stoves Stoves with an adjustable plate for widening or narrowing an opening and regulating the draught.
vereas Whereas.
indentures Sealed agreement or contract, usually for apprenticeship.
this very unusual gymnastic performance A fine piece of irony to emphasize the appearance as distinct from the reality – the clean shirt into which Oliver struggles will increase his opportunities of being sold to Gamfield.
for there was quite enough water in it already An ironic reminder that all the paupers' supplies are watered down.
obeisance Bow of respect.
A moral revolution Dickens often uses exclamation marks or apostrophes in order to reflect pomposity, as he does here. The revolution is later to be permanent in its effects, when Bumble is taken over by Mrs Corney.

Chapter 4

The Board makes a decision to send Oliver to sea, but Bumble has a fortuitous meeting with Mr Sowerberry, the undertaker. The latter discusses the incidence of death and the ignorance of juries. The two men arrange for Oliver to go to Sowerberry; Oliver breaks down when Bumble takes him, and we feel that the beadle is himself a little moved. Arrived at the undertaker's Oliver is pushed into the kitchen, to feed on the scraps left by the dog. He is then led off to sleep amid the coffins.

Commentary

There is a kind of grim humour in the exchange between Sowerberry and Bumble which reveals a cynical attitude towards life, or rather, death. There is further irony in the 'porochial' seal representing the Good Samaritan, and the ensuing and insensitive account of the tradesman who died because he didn't have the common 'necessaries' of life. Oliver's tears show that he has not yet been brutalized or made insensitive by his way of life, and the hint that Bumble too is moved shows Dickens presenting character with rather more depth than we might at first consider. Oliver's deprivation is more practically shown by his reaction to the mention of meat. Here Dickens's propagandist tone is evident – devouring the dog's scraps, Oliver, treated like an animal, behaves like one. This carries its own indictment of the system.

In great families, when an advantageous place cannot be obtained The author in his own voice, the omniscient mode of addressing the reader that occurs throughout the novel.
professional jocosity i.e. humorous, waggish, in order to promote business.
an ingenious little model of a patent coffin Almost a piece of advertising, but very ironic if we look forward and remember that it is a 'sneeze-box' which traps the Dodger.
So are the coffins i.e. they are small because the paupers are so wasted away.
The people who have been better off . . . are the first to sink A basic psychological truth – the respectable feel the degradation of their loss of position more than those who have never had one.
The die is the same as the porochial seal – the Good Samaritan An incisive piece of irony – the parish, the beadle, the Board can hardly be equated with the symbol of the true Christian.
the relieving officer i.e. the official charged with the care of the poor.
I wish some well-fed philosopher Again the favourite device of the author moralizing in his own voice – but here the social (and moral) concern is very strong indeed. The implication is that boys are reduced to animals by the inhumanity of men.

Chapter 5

Oliver is oppressed by the atmosphere of death in the shop, and almost wishes he too were dead. Next morning, he is awakened by a kicking at the door and meets the charity boy Noah Claypole. Oliver accidentally breaks a window in taking down the shutters. When he has been there about a month, Sowerberry proposes to his 'vixenish' wife that Oliver shall be a mute for the 'children's practice'. The very next day Bumble comes to the undertaker's to arrange for a funeral.

Oliver and Sowerberry go to the house where the woman lies dead; and the poverty and degradation of the area are described: 'The very rats, which here and there lay putrefying in its rottenness, were hideous with famine' (p.81). Oliver is appalled and frightened by what he sees. The husband is raving hysterically over the body, and the starving, staring children are crying bitterly. The old woman is a grotesque, asking for a cloak and bread and wine in order to follow her daughter to the grave. The following day is the day of the funeral, and Oliver runs by Sowerberry's side. They have to wait for more than an hour for the clergyman to conduct the perfunctory service; the husband collapses at the graveside, and Oliver and Sowerberry return to the shop.

Commentary

One of the most moving chapters in the book, and something of a study in social realism. Before that, however, there is a fine focus on the sensitive child and the insensitive way in which he is treated. Claypole immediately emerges as a bully, while Mr Sowerberry is the classic case of the henpecked husband. However, he shows some astuteness in handling his wife over Oliver becoming a mute. The description of the town and the state of the interior of the house where the woman lies dead shows Dickens intent upon exposing the social evils of his time. It also shows a superb sense of realism in the reaction of the old woman and the husband, the latter almost hysterical while the former has an 'idiotic leer' and has obviously been driven mad by her daughter's death from starvation. The burial, and everything associated with it, is degrading, even down to the hurried entrance of the clergyman. There is some insight into

Sowerberry, who has got 'used to it' and recommends Oliver to do the same.

like high-shouldered ghosts Dickens is the great creator of atmosphere – particularly that of fear and the supernatural – seen here in the reactions of a child to his frightening new surroundings.
two mutes Mourners hired for the occasion.
like a grave Notice how this simile reflects Oliver's imagination.
charity-boy Charity schools provided inadequate, sub-standard education for the children of the very poor.
with edifying gravity i.e. morally improving seriousness (very ironic tone – Noah has no improving qualities, as we are soon to see).
yellow smalls Breeches, from 'small-clothes': knee-breeches.
leathers Breeches.
It shows us what a beautiful thing human nature may be Another direct moral comment, this time on the evil inherent in man regardless of status.
unpropitious aspect i.e. an unfavourable look or appearance, a short altercation of less than three-quarters of an hour's duration. An argument – heavy irony on the time it takes.
functionary i.e. Bumble.
firmly bound for seven years i.e. the length of the apprenticeship.
concurrent testimony i.e. agreeing evidence.
The kennel From the Old French *canel* – gutter.
she died in the dark One of the most moving sequences in the early part of the novel – a fine example of Dickens's ability to write graphically and to create the sordid atmosphere of human deprivation.
bier The movable stand on which the coffin (or corpse) is taken to the grave.

Chapter 6

Oliver is now in regular service as an admired mute. Noah is very jealous of Oliver's elevation, tantalizes him and abuses Oliver's mother. Oliver fells him, whereupon Noah cries out and Charlotte and Mrs Sowerberry set upon Oliver. Later Noah leaves to get Mr Bumble.

Commentary

This is a dramatic and human chapter. In the first instance, there is the focus on Oliver as mute, a kind of commercial exploitation of death, with Dickens's voice commenting ironically on the behaviour and the ostentation of some people in grief. The moral of the chapter is that even the worm will turn. Oliver does, on the insult to his mother, and here Dickens portrays him more as a symbol of goodness, morality and right thinking rather than as a real boy. Nonetheless Dickens generates considerable excitement in the fight, and there is a grotesque element of comedy too as they all set upon Oliver. The bully is exposed as a sniveller, and Charlotte and Mrs Sowerberry are exposed as vindictive creatures intent on exaggerating. There is a farcical and graphic immediacy about Noah's flight to Mr Bumble.

ingenious speculation i.e. clever idea.
equanimity of demeanour i.e. balance and control.
muffin-cap The cap – a flat one – worn by boys from charity schools.
as the hungry pig was, when he was shut up by mistake A sort of folk-simile of a kind much used in the 19th century.
And now, I come to a very important passage in Oliver's history Here, the use of the *intimate* author's voice, almost as if he is confiding a secret to the reader – which indeed he is!
Tol de rol lol lol A kind of 'tell us the old old story' mockery of what Oliver is saying.
Bridewell The house of correction, or a prison.
His breast heaved; his attitude was erect Note the superb economy of the style, used to convey the sharp economy of the action to come – Oliver's assault on Noah.
millingtary i.e. the military, the soldiers (doubtless Noah would feel more secure with their arrival).
You can hold a knife to that black eye i.e. the coldness of the blade.

Chapter 7

Noah reports Oliver's assault, with suitable distortion. Bumble is thereupon ordered by the gentleman in the white waistcoat to go up and flog Oliver. Bumble comes to the conclusion that Oliver's behaviour can be traced to the fact that he has been fed on meat, and he advocates keeping Oliver in the cellar for a day or two to starve him down, as he puts it. When Sowerberry arrives he is obliged by overwhelming domestic opinion to beat Oliver; when the latter retires to 'bed' that night he breaks down. He ties his few articles of clothing together and waits for the dawn; then sets off, stopping by the cottage where he had been 'brought up by hand' by Mrs Mann. There he takes leave of one of his former little companions, Dick, who kisses and blesses him – a blessing that Oliver cherishes, and does not forget.

Commentary

Noah demonstrates that he is a ham actor but, since Bumble is too, the appearance of the gentleman in the white waistcoat fortuitously gives them a chance to perform and distort Oliver's mood and character. The primitive idea of 'parochial flagellation' is decided on. But it is Sowerberry himself who is, so to speak, put on the spot, his having to flog Oliver to satisfy Mrs Sowerberry being evidence of the nature of domestic politics which rules decisions and actions. After the pathos of Oliver's breakdown there is the excitement of his surreptitious flight and the additional pathos – some would say exaggerated sentiment – of Oliver's farewell to Dick. Although the two boys are stereotypes, and although there is distortion, their parting is none the less moving.

sanguinary onset i.e. bloody attack.
this comes of being liberal Mrs Sowerberry's complacency is here being subjected to the now familiar Dickensian irony – we remember that her 'liberality' consists of giving Oliver the dog's scraps.

Chapter 8

Oliver finds that he is some 75 miles from London. He walks 20 miles that day, 12 the next, sleeping in the open. At one stage he begs by running after a coach, but the passengers are too mean to give him their promised half-pence. Oliver, like Joe in *Bleak House* later, is compelled to move on by threats. He reaches Barnet on the seventh day, and sits by the roadside, his feet bleeding. A strange boy approaches him, befriends him, and offers to buy him food, all the while talking in a strange dialect. Oliver eats, and Jack Dawkins tells him that he knows of an old man in London who will give him shelter. Jack is known as The Artful Dodger; they set off, arriving in London at night, passing through the dirty streets, with filthy children rolling in the gutters. After the Dodger provides the password, they enter a house and go up the stairs and into a back room. The 'villainous-looking' Fagin and the interior of the room are described; there are a number of boys drinking spirits 'with the air of middle-aged men', and Oliver has some gin and water and falls asleep.

Commentary

Oliver's journey in want may be compared with Sikes's journey in fear later in the novel. In both there are superb graphic description and realism, a continuing sense of atmosphere. There is irony in the fact that Oliver feels that he will be safe in London. A further instance of almost casual inhumanity is seen in the attitude of the coach-passengers towards Oliver's pathetic attempts to keep up, and an indication of the severity of the laws against poverty is given in the notice about beggars being jailed.

There are two instances of human kindness as compensation. The Dodger makes an immediate impact through the richness of his language and the flamboyance of his personality. Note that whatever his motives, he is at least kind to Oliver. Dickens's description of him conveys his vivid eccentricity, his loveable – and pathetic – grotesqueness. Note the meticulous account of the Dodger's route into London, and the portrayal of a world dominated by squalor, drunkenness and crime. Dickens is master of low-life slang. Fagin's room, though filthy, symbolizes a warmth of life unknown to Oliver, while the description of the 'merry old gentleman' adds another positive grotesque to the list of characters in this novel. Note, too, the many hints that this is a den of thieves.

which brought Oliver's heart into his mouth – very often the only thing he had there Dickens never allows us to forget Oliver's state – and he is preparing us for the 'humanity' of the Dodger and the warmth and comfort *by contrast* of Fagin's den when placed beside the previous experiences Oliver has suffered.

turnpike man i.e. the collector at the gate set across the road – drivers of carts, for example, had to pay a toll at these gates before they could continue their journey.

Hullo, my covey! What's the row? Strictly speaking, 'Hallo, old chap. What's the matter?'.

four feet six ... in his bluchers This stress on his size makes the Dodger at once grotesque and pathetic. He is still a 'little' boy whom circumstances have forced into precocious adulthood. For the note on the type of boots – bluchers – which the Dodger is wearing, see the Penguin English Library edition p.487.

Beak's order i.e. a magistrate's order.
my flash com-pan-i-on The Dodger is often heavily sarcastic – Oliver is hardly 'gaudy or showy'.
how green i.e. innocent.
mill i.e. treadmill.
a Stone Jug Prison.
the wind's low with people i.e. when money is short.
acos i.e. because.
I'm at a low-water-mark myself i.e. I haven't got much money.
one bob and a magpie One shilling and a halfpenny.
I'll fork out and stump I'll spend my money – and stand treat.
chandler's shop i.e. a dealer in candles, oil, soap – and groceries.
fourpenny bran Sounds like the Dodger's pronunciation of 'brown'. Slang for a 'loaf'.
falling to i.e. beginning to eat.
Don't fret your eyelids Don't worry yourself.
By no means. Certainly not The Dodger often speaks the reverse of what he means quite deliberately, as a means of exaggerating the effect.
protégé A person to whom another is protector or patron.
sobriquet Nickname or assumed name.
Islington . . . the Angel . . . St John's road The interested student who acquires an A to Z or a large-scale map of London will be able to trace the route and find the places mentioned here and in the succeeding pages.
Plummy and slam! (The pass-word). Probably 'a very good trick'.
Greenland We have already seen that 'green' means 'innocent', and both ironically and realistically the word suits Oliver.
the wipes Handkerchiefs.

Chapter 9

The next morning Oliver is half awake, half asleep; he listens to Fagin talking to himself, and watches him produce a box and examine the trinkets in it. When he realizes that Oliver is awake he is at first angry, but then tells him that it is a little property he has put aside for his old age. The Dodger returns accompanied by his friend Charley Bates – they have been stealing. Oliver watches the game of pick-pocketing played by the old gentleman and the boys, and then takes part in it himself. He is 'green', and gets further practice with Fagin when the others have gone out to 'work'.

Commentary

Atmosphere of mystery as Oliver watches Fagin without being clear what he is saying or doing. Fagin is in fact pondering on and praising the idea of honour among thieves. Fagin's obsession and his neurosis are well in evidence in his initial reaction to Oliver. The latter is an innocent and his 'greenness' is cause for humour. The game is a superb anticipation of what is to come later when Oliver is suspected of pick-pocketing – it has a typical Dickensian theatricality and verve about it here. The irony embraces the fact that everything is being seen – like the 'very nice girls', Bet and Nancy – through the innocent eyes of Oliver.

corporeal associate i.e. the body, the framework.
Clever dogs i.e. cunning.
Staunch to the last i.e. true, did not betray.
Never told the old parson i.e. the prison chaplain, who would hear the last words or confessions of thieves/murderers before they were hanged.
loosened the knot or kept the drop up i.e. the hangman's noose – the drop is the platform withdrawn from under the feet of the condemned man.
to play booty To betray.
Lined i.e. having money in them.
marked them well Part of Fagin's humour – he wants Oliver to remove any means of identifying the owners!
a great deal of colour in their faces They were rouged – but perhaps the 'colour' is also as a result of their drinking too much.
As there is no doubt they were Heavy irony – they are 'nice', undoubtedly, to their male customers (Dickens was later to write that Nancy was a prostitute) – further evidence of Oliver's innocence!
pad the hoof i.e. go out for a walk.

Chapter 10

Oliver is in Fagin's room, picking the marks out of the handkerchiefs; after a while he is taken out by Charley and the Dodger. The latter, seeing an old gentleman at a bookstall, steals his handkerchief. Oliver, seeing this, is frightened and runs. In the ensuing hue and cry Oliver is chased, hurled to the ground, and the old gentleman and a police officer arrive on the scene. Oliver is dragged by his jacket-collar to the magistrate's court.

Commentary

Dickens's sense of irony is shown in the 'stern morality' of Fagin and the continued emphasis on Oliver's innocence as the boys descend on their prey. Notice the dramatic onset of right morality in Oliver! Also contributing to the sheer speed of the narrative in this chapter is the opportunism of the Dodger and Charley Bates, who join in the pursuit of Oliver. The author notes the passion for hunting 'something', and distinguishes between the bullying and undiscriminating crowd and the compassionate nature of the old gentleman who has been robbed.

what branch of manufacture he would be instructed in first Another ironic description of the 'occupation' of the boys.
areas Sunken courts railed off from the pavement and giving access to the basements of houses.
A prime plant i.e. ideal for stealing from.
depredator One who steals or pillages.
Stop thief! This whole sequence should be studied carefully for the insight it gives into Dickens's stylistic methods – the graphic narrative, the sense of atmosphere, the feel of the chase. All are conveyed by a sudden switch into the present tense.
Although Oliver had been brought up by philosophers Irony in high-flown language to emphasize that Oliver was *not* brought up by any such people.
panting with exhaustion The effect conveyed is that of a hunted *animal* – and the effect is deliberate.
Punch This is a reference to a Punch and Judy show, since the first number of the magazine was not published until 1841.
Give him a little air Again the graphic immediacy, this time conveyed by the use of dialogue from the witnesses. Dickens has a superb sense of the dramatic, as we shall see when we read on.
(who is generally the last person to arrive in such cases) The favourite Dickensian device of including an ironic aside to the reading audience in a bracket.

Revision questions on Chapters 1–10

1 Write a character sketch of Mr Bumble as he appears in these chapters.

2 By reference to the text, give instances of the author's use of his own voice.

3 Compare and contrast conditions in the workhouse with those in Fagin's den.

4 Bring out the quality of Dickens's humour with reference to the Artful Dodger or Noah Claypole.

5 Write an account of Dickens's ability to create *atmosphere* in any two or three scenes of these chapters.

6 'Oliver is a symbol, not a real boy.' Discuss.

Chapter 11

The old gentleman is intrigued by Oliver's face. Oliver is brought before the magistrate, the infamous Mr Fang. The latter is reading about himself in a newspaper, and soon demonstrates his incompetence, brutality and sheer ignorance; Oliver is only saved from three months' imprisonment by the appearance and intervention of the owner of the bookstall, who has seen the whole incident. Mr Brownlow, the old gentleman, is seething with rage after being reprimanded by Fang, but afterwards takes Oliver to his own home.

Commentary

Note the clues which are being laid here, particularly with regard to Oliver's real identity. For the original of Mr Fang, see the section on *Background and setting*, but also note Dickens's account of the arbitrary processes of the law in the insistence on Oliver being charged. Dickens also indicts the filth of prison cells, the self-importance and the power of the magistrate. Owing to the testimony of the bookstall-owner, justice finally triumphs almost in spite of the man who should be dispensing it. Dickens, as ever, is on the side of the oppressed and innocent, though again we feel that Fang is perhaps more caricature than reality. There is something comic in the way he very *nearly* has Mr Brownlow charged with stealing, since the latter still has the book he was reading, but had not bought, in his hand.

fogle-hunter i.e. after the handkerchiefs.
Newgate The notorious London prison.
There is something in that boy's face Dickens loves a mystery – and here is the first clue planted in the reader's mind about Oliver's birth.
he might have brought an action against his countenance for libel, and have recovered heavy damages Note how the legal image is

applied to the man whose legal actions are an abuse of the system – a further ironic commentary on the nature of his actions.

commending him i.e. bringing him to the attention of (the Secretary of State for the Home Department). Further irony.

mandate Directive, order.

Chapter 12

Oliver is ill, and recovers after a long rest, during which time he is nursed by the old gentleman's housekeeper, Mrs Bedwin. He has had a bad fever, and after the doctor has called he sleeps again. When he wakes he looks at the picture on the wall of the room, thinking that the lady portrayed in it has a beautiful face – he even feels that she wants to speak to him. Mr Brownlow comes in to talk to Oliver, and notices that the boy resembles the young woman in the portrait.

Commentary

Vivid imagery (see below) indicates the wasting effect of Oliver's fever but the overall purpose of this chapter is to contrast deprivation and criminality with the kindness found in the Brownlow household – an assertion of faith in the goodness of human nature which is *not* degraded by social conditions and maladministration. The atmosphere of the sick-room and Oliver's passing through the valley of the shadow of death is realistically conveyed. Once again, the clue as to the boy's birth receives emphasis: Oliver's interaction with the portrait is overlaid with sentiment, and there is some irony in the fact that Mr Brownlow is unable to place the familiar features he finds in Oliver's face. The discovery that the resemblance lies in the picture above Oliver's head provides a fitting climax to the chapter.

The worm does not his work more surely Note that Dickens achieves a form of unity through the imagery – here we are reminded of the dead woman visited by Sowerberry and Oliver, and the man's fears.

I almost feel as if she had Dickens begins to plant the clues that lead to the later revelations of Oliver's birth.

three hundred and fifty paupers, at the lowest computation i.e. at the lowest reckoning or calculation. The main area of Dickens's attack – the *administration* of the Poor Law – is constantly referred to by analogy, so that the reader will not forget.

the machine for taking likenesses This is the process of heliography.

as if it was alive, and wanted to speak to me, but couldn't Another indication of Oliver's sensitivity – and another clue that his mother is symbolically present.
expedition Speed.
some hydraulic process which we are not sufficiently philosophical to be in a condition to explain Occasionally Dickens is needlessly verbose, as here, where he really means to emphasize the naturalness of human response as distinct from theory – that tears freely given in sympathy are worth more than abstract thought.
There was its living copy The final clue in a chapter that has been generous in providing them.

Chapter 13

A return to Charley and the Dodger, with the former greatly amused at Oliver's plight: but Fagin indicates that he is not at all amused, and soundly berates the boys for what has happened. Sikes enters, and now it is Fagin's turn to be shouted at. When the two girls arrive, Nancy is virtually coerced into going to the police office to enquire for her 'young brother'. She enters into the spirit of the pretence, acting the part well in preparation, much to the amusement of the others. When she goes to the office she learns of course that Oliver has been taken home by Mr Brownlow. Fagin, 'greatly excited', sets in train the search for Oliver.

Commentary

The narrative switch to Charley Bates and the Dodger is very effective, Charley's humour being matched by the Dodger's 'intellectual countenance'. Fagin reveals a surprising capacity for violence but the most effective moment in the chapter is the entrance of Sikes, euphemistically described as 'an engaging ruffian'. Again the theatrical talent of Dickens is evident, with Sikes engaging in dumb show, Fagin shrewdly entering upon a little blackmail on Sikes, and all of them pondering upon whether Oliver has 'peached'. All this makes for narrative tension and Nancy's assumption of her part carries with it a curious irony as she acts out the loss of her 'poor, dear, sweet, innocent little brother'. Later greatly moved by that innocence, she does her best to preserve it, though there is as yet no indication of the moral side to her character.

34 Oliver Twist

Dickens uses the scene at the police station to cite yet another example of the inhumanity of Fang – the locking up of the flute player, and other poor vagrants. The chapter again ends on a note of excitement as Nancy and the Dodger set off to get Oliver back.

the good lady's proceedings Here Dickens is personifying 'Nature' – that aspect of it which demonstrates, through the behaviour of the Dodger and Charley, that self-preservation is the mainspring of human action.
like unto those in which drunken men Dickens is indulging an elaborate simile, rather in the manner of Fielding, at the expense of 'philosophers' whose thoughts are imprecisely put.
apostrophe Exclamatory address.
Toor rul lol loo, gammon and spinnage The Dodger is indulging his own version of the nursery rhyme 'A Frog he would a-wooing go', adding his own interpretation to Charley of what he thinks Fagin's response will be to the loss of Oliver.
trivet Iron bracket for hooking on the bars of the grate.
the traps The police.
I'd have settled somebody I'd have killed somebody.
he done the River Company every quarter He has not paid the water-rate to the New River Company.
warmint Vermin.
without a set of fetters to garnish them i.e. leg irons to set them off. The implication is, of course, that Sikes should be imprisoned.
belcher handkerchief Belcher was the famous bare-knuckle fighter who died in 1811, and this is a kind of scarf named after him.
covetous, avaricious, in-sa-ti-a-ble old fence Occasionally Dickens errs in emphasis: this language is almost too good for Sikes to use. He does not repeat it again, but sticks to the earthy abusive idiom of his type. A fence is a receiver of stolen goods.
a curiosity of ugliness in a glass bottle Emphasizing that Fagin deviates from the normal – just as specimens of deviations from the normal are sometimes preserved as curiosities.
as you do when you blab The implication is that Fagin talks, gives the game away, when he wishes to.
tying an imaginary knot under his left ear i.e. to signify hanging.
You're blowed upon You're betrayed.
the old gentleman's shoulders were shrugged up to his ears A wonderfully visual way of showing that Fagin is saying that it is beyond his means to control what happens or is revealed.
done at the office i.e. the police office.
a red gown, green boots and yellow curl-papers A sufficient indication of their occupation – Bet and Nancy are prostitutes.
genivine i.e. genuine.

Oh, my brother! My poor, dear, sweet, innocent little brother! One of the main stylistic effects in *Oliver Twist* is Dickens's use of theatrical situations and images. Theatre, music-hall, melodrama, getting up plays himself – these were the love of his life. There is frequent reference to acting in this novel, generally of an ironic nature, as here. Acting like Nancy's is the appearance that conceals the reality or truth, and Dickens is much concerned with this in *Oliver Twist*.
encomiums   Exclamations of praise.
Nolly   Short for 'Oliver'.
the domicile   i.e. where he (Fagin) was living.
the other ken   i.e. the other hiding-place.
stop his windpipe   Prevent him forcefully from talking.

Chapter 14

When Oliver finally recovers he finds that the picture has been removed from the wall on Mr Brownlow's orders. But the days of his recovery are happy ones as he is cared for by Mrs Bedwin; he has a long talk with Mr Brownlow, and begs not to be sent back to Fagin. Then Mr Grimwig joins Mr Brownlow. Mr Brownlow believes strongly in Oliver, because of his appearance and manner. Mr Grimwig affects not to. In fact the two old gentlemen, though close friends, enjoy opposing each other. Oliver volunteers to take some books and a five-pound note to the bookseller for Mr Brownlow – while the latter and Mr Grimwig argue as to whether or not Oliver will return.

Commentary

Notice the solicitude for Oliver which Mr Brownlow and Mrs Bedwin show by removing the picture, though this is symbolic too – his mother no longer watches over him. Oliver symbolically also rids himself of his past by discarding his old clothes. Dickens makes some critical remarks about authors, while Mr Brownlow, despite adverse experiences, represents faith in the goodness of human nature. Grimwig proves to be in the line of eccentrics – his 'I'll eat my head, sir', and his suspicion of malice from the surgeon on finding the orange peel in his path, provide a rich source of humour, as does his ingrained habit of contradiction. That and chance provide the dramatic ending to the chapter with Oliver's departure and non-return.

expatiated i.e. enlarged upon.
cribbage A card game for two, three or four persons.
as smart as sixpence Proverbial saying meaning 'as good as new, we'll brighten you up'.
quartos A book consisting of sheets of paper folded twice.
I have not made a coffin of my heart Again we are reminded of the death of the poor woman whom Sowerberry buries.
nankeen Made of a kind of cotton cloth, originally from Nanking (China).
poor surgeon's-friend i.e. the orange peel that causes the accident, and hence gives the doctor a patient!
his infernal red lamp with the pantomime-light The night-time sign of a doctor.
Mealy i.e. pale, the colour of flour.
with the voice of a pilot A pilot, accustomed to giving orders in rough weather, would need a loud voice.
counting the plate at night i.e. checking to see if all the silver and valuable articles were still there and had not been stolen.
in slight expectation, with the watch between them Fine humour with a strong visual quality – ridiculous, but at the same time pathetic.

Chapter 15

Sikes is brooding in the low pub in Little Saffron Hill and managing to maltreat his dog at the same time; Fagin enters and passes money to Sikes. Nancy is eating in another bar, but later she leaves and finds Oliver near the bookstall. According to the pre-arranged and pre-acted plan, Nancy claims Oliver as her brother, aided and abetted by the sudden appearance of Sikes. Oliver is carried off to the other 'ken' while Mrs Bedwin and the two obdurate old gentlemen remain at home.

Commentary

Immediate contrast is established with this return to the sordid. Sikes's capacity for violence, an important ingredient in his character, is stressed, but so also is the humanitarian side which damns the government which 'lets a man kill a dog how he likes'. There is a nice balance established with Sikes's and Fagin's mutual blackmailing. Note the interaction between Barney and Fagin which goes unnoticed by Sikes but which increases the dramatic tension, as does the look from Sikes to Nancy to warn her that she is talking too much. There is a terrible irony in Nancy's rescuing Oliver from what she calls 'a set of thieves and bad characters'. They set off with Sikes and Bull's-eye in menacing attendance, the further irony being the unwitting collusion and approval of the bystanders.

pewter measure i.e. the beer mug.
adage Traditional maxim, proverb.
unless it's behind a nightcap i.e. the cap placed on the head of the prisoner by the executioner.
Stow that gammon Stop that nonsense.
Jerk the tinkler Ring the bell.
Dot a shoul Not a soul.
Dobdoy but Biss Dadsy Nobody but Miss Nancy.
bid havid i.e. been having.
on the scent This commonplace image links up with the previous 'hunt' of Oliver after the Dodger has stolen Mr Brownlow's 'wiper'.
Hue-and-Cry The police gazette.
sich Such.
mind him i.e. guard him, see that he doesn't escape.

Chapter 16

Sikes and Nancy press on with Oliver, with Bull's-eye in attendance. As they pass on, the clock strikes eight, and Nancy ponders on the fate of their fellow criminals who are awaiting execution. Oliver now realizes that Nancy is suffering. Eventually, after a long walk, they reach the other 'ken'; here the boys mock Oliver's superior clothes, and Sikes is quick to pocket the five-pound note. Oliver tries to run away, and Nancy becomes hysterical and warns Sikes not to set the dog on him. There follows a terrible row in which Nancy reveals that she possesses a core of goodness: a moral sense that has defied the corruption of years. Finally she faints; Oliver is made to change back into his old clothes; and Miss Betsy arrives in time to bring Nancy back to her senses.

Commentary

Sikes's brutality is stressed, particularly his setting the dog to threaten Oliver. Nancy reacts by showing her capacity for sympathy with those who are suffering, which ultimately leads to her doing what she can for Oliver. There is something dreadful in the laughter of Charley Bates and the simulated obsequiousness of Fagin towards Oliver in his superior clothes. Oliver's sufferings on account of Mr Brownlow's thinking him a thief are extreme. Sikes shows an astute knowledge of psychology in asserting that Mr Brownlow will not take any action against Oliver. Nancy's responses show her to be hysterical and, perhaps because we have had little preparation for them, somewhat unrealistic. Nevertheless, there is a fine dramatic quality about her passion and the scene with Fagin and Sikes, while Charley Bates waxes humorous and eccentric as he returns Oliver's old clothes to him. Greed rules; the new ones will doubtless fetch good money.

Bartlemy time The feast of St Bartholomew occurs on 24 August.
shopped i.e. to be informed on and hence imprisoned.
pitch over i.e. throw over (the prison wall).
down in the mouth Depressed.
a glim A light.
it is such a jolly game Charley is here mocking superior speech as well as superior clothes.
viewed him round and round ... a great number of low bows Note that this is another aspect of the theatrical appearance and reality theme – and here it is all done, very effectively, in mime.
saturnine ... assiduity Gloomy temperament ... great thoroughness.
togs Clothes.
heavy swell cut i.e. in the height of superior fashion – dandyish.
soft-hearted psalm-singers i.e. Christians who are easily imposed upon or easily moved to charitable action.
I shall put that mark on some of you Probably 'I shall kill you', but it could mean that she will give them away – ironic in view of what does happen.
you are acting beautifully So is Fagin, who says this to Nancy, but who suspects that she is not acting at all.
imprecation Curse.

Chapter 17

There is a narrative switch here, and we find Mr Bumble visiting Mrs Mann: he tells her that he is going to London. There is a harrowing interview with Dick, who wants to let Oliver know how much he has thought of him. Next day Bumble sets off for London, and the evening finds him enjoying a meal; he reads of Mr Brownlow's offer of a five-guinea reward for the finding of Oliver Twist. He goes to see Brownlow and, as we should expect, gives Oliver a bad character. But Mrs Bedwin refuses to believe any ill of 'her boy'.

Commentary

The opening of the chapter has the author defining his method of alternating the comic and the tragic scenes and at the same time indicating that this kind of alternation is true to life. Irony plays over Bumble in 'the full bloom and pride of beadlehood'. His exchange with Mrs Mann, though comic and indeed grotesque, reveals his hard-heartedness, and with the appearance of Dick – 'The scanty parish dress, the livery of his misery' – who is obviously dying, he is moved to further condemn Oliver. Note the speed of the narrative once Mr Bumble reads of the reward for Oliver; again greed is the motive. There is irony in the fact that Bumble learns too late that if he had given Oliver a good character he would have earned much more money.

It is the custom on the stage, in all good murderous melodramas, to present the tragic and the comic scenes, in as regular alternation, as the layers of red and white in a side of streaky bacon This is a fine definition of Dickens's own method in *Oliver Twist*, and the student should read the next three paragraphs closely, since they reflect the use of the author's own voice in explanation and judgement – the presence, as Kathleen Tillotson has rightly called it, of the teller in the tale.
seneschal Steward of a medieval great house.
vassals Slaves or servants.
and roam about in company, carolling perpetually An ironic tone, which describes what he calls, in the next paragraph, the 'mimic life' of the theatre.
'Drat that beadle . . . it *is* a pleasure, this is! A finely economical instance of the hypocrisy of human nature – another underlining of the appearance/reality theme.
worrit Worry.
to send them paupers in carts Further evidence, if it were needed, of Mrs Mann's humanity!
if we can throw 'em upon another parish Again notice that Dickens is keeping up his attack on the administration of the Poor Law – the various authorities trying to shift responsibility for the paupers on to one another.
out-dacious . . . demogalized them all Mr Bumble means 'audacious' and 'demoralized', but he hasn't quite got the Dodger's ability to colour his malapropisms with individual verve.
I never see such a hardened little wretch Here is the appearance of the words and the reality of pathetic innocence they malign.
a retrospective manner i.e. to help him think back.

Chapter 18

Fagin lectures Oliver on the sin of ingratitude, but after a week or so the boy is left alone and is able to explore the dilapidated house in which he finds himself. On a later occasion he cleans the Dodger's boots for him, and the Dodger and Charley try to influence Oliver into putting himself completely under Fagin's wing. Their philosophy is quite simple: watches and handkerchiefs are there for the taking. Later still Fagin tells Oliver stories of robberies, and there is a constant return to the handkerchief game.

Commentary

Note the brutality of Fagin in threatening Oliver with the ultimate punishment of hanging; ironically that demise is to be his. The state of the house is a symbol for the decayed state of the criminals who now live there. The Dodger and Charley Bates are naturally fluent, and their language has the ring of truth. Their failure to corrupt Oliver shows how intent Dickens is on making the boy a symbol of goodness. Chitling represents the fact that crime does not pay, since he has just been released from prison. Oliver's laughing at what he is told despite himself – Dickens says that he is in the Jew's toils – humanizes him to the extent that we feel he just *might* be corrupted.

customary avocations i.e. usual occupations, stealing.
in his philanthropy Practical benevolence, goodness of heart – an ironic way of describing Fagin's capacity to corrupt.
as if he had lived inside the ball of St Paul's Cathedral A fine imaginative analogy to define Oliver's imprisonment.
japanning his trotter-cases Immediately defined as 'cleaning his boots'.
tinctured, for the nonce, with a spice of romance Flavoured, for the time being. The Dodger is a little softened.
prig Thief.
downiest one of the lot i.e. the most cunning.
wittles Victuals, supplies.
in the very next leap-year . . . the forty-second Tuesday in Trinity-week Charley is always given to fanciful expression, implying that he can pick his time when to retire on the proceeds of his stealing.
take any pride out of yourself The Dodger means, ironically, 'haven't you got any self-respect?'.
made our lucky i.e. got away, made our escape.

you precious flat Fool.
scragged i.e. hanged.
prime company i.e. first-rate.
fogles and tickers Handkerchiefs and watches.
lies in a nutshell i.e. it's the truth.
time i.e. sentence.
having worn the regimentals i.e. prison garb.
fumigating Disinfecting with fumes.
no remedy against the County i.e. you couldn't do anything about it.

Chapter 19

Fagin makes for Bethnal Green to see Sikes; he drinks with him and Nancy, and they discuss the practicalities of the 'crib at Chertsey'. Fagin is trying to provoke Sikes into action. We learn that 'Flash' Toby Crackit has achieved little in the area and that the job will have to be done from the outside, thus involving the use of a boy to get in. The obvious choice is Oliver, who is small enough to get through the aperture. The details of the journey are sketched, and Nancy is to go and get Oliver.

Commentary

The night is atmospheric of the evil that is being contemplated. The dialogue between Sikes and Fagin underlines this, and greed urges them to take the risk of using Oliver. Due caution is displayed with regard to Nancy, and Sikes inveighs against society which makes it difficult to get hold of the right kind of boy. There is a grim humour in this. Fagin obviously has an intuitive feeling that Nancy is not to be trusted, again ironic in view of what is to happen later. Fagin is calculating psychologically on making Oliver 'Ours for his life' by corrupting him in this way. When he leaves he deludes himself that Nancy is true. The chapter concludes with Fagin almost touched by the sight of the sleeping Oliver, a rare glimpse of the man's humanity.

like some loathsome reptile One of the strongest similes used of Fagin.
some rich offal for a meal The above image is here continued, the effect being to stress the subhumanity of Fagin.
a 'life-preserver' A short stick with a heavily loaded end.
crib House.
into a line . . . got over i.e. they can't be brought round to the burglar's way of thinking – they cannot be bribed.

flash Dandified.
the other plant i.e. planned swindle, criminal scheme.
feared the game was up i.e. that they would not be successful.
fifty shiners extra Fifty guineas.
let it come off as soon . . . Let's do it quickly . . .
centre-bit i.e. for making cylindrical holes.
lagged Transported.
arning Earning.
Keep the game a-going! Never say die! Clichés indicating unswerving loyalty.
snoozing about Common Garden i.e. sleeping (for want of anything to do or anywhere to go).
leg-bail Escape.
bring off the swag Carrying away the proceeds.
get off the stones an hour arter daybreak Leave an hour after dawn.
keep the melting-pot ready Used for melting down silver or even gold plate so that no stolen goods can be traced.
The man against the child, for a bag of gold Fagin is calculating on Sikes having a greater claim on Nancy's loyalty than Oliver has.

Chapter 20

Fagin tells Oliver that he is going to Sikes. He leaves him a book to read, which turns out to be an account of the lives of the great criminals. When Nancy comes for him it is obvious that she is overwrought, and she tells Oliver that she will do all that she can for him. She takes him to Sikes; the latter, of course, threatens Oliver, impresses upon him what to do if anything goes wrong, and then has supper. Oliver hopes for a look from Nancy, but she continues to sit unseeing in front of the fire.

Commentary

Oliver's reading matter is something dear to Dickens, who is always obsessed with crime and stories of lurid terror. But here it is quite deliberate – the book is Fagin's Bible, and he is the great criminal who is to suffer anguish in the end. There is further insight into Nancy's nature and suffering, her bruises clear evidence of Sikes's brutality. Narrative expectation is aroused by the preparations.

bantered i.e. joked, teased.
when his own is up i.e. when he is angry.
You are hedged round and round i.e. you are trapped, you cannot escape.

Every word from you is a blow for me Nancy means that she will suffer at Sikes's hands if Oliver says anything to incense him.
hackney-cabriolet Light, two-wheeled, hooded one-horse chaise.
That's the time of day The right way.
of a old hat for waddin i.e. for keeping the powder or shot compact in a gun.
when it's blowing up i.e. when they are scolding and ranting.
on active service Ironic use of the term: here meaning about to be engaged in burglary.
mending the fire i.e. keeping it going.

Revision questions on Chapters 11–20

1 Show how Dickens makes effective use of contrast by an account of any two chapters here.

2 Give some account of the part played by Nancy in these chapters.

3 Compare and contrast Mr Brownlow and Mr Grimwig.

4 Write a description of the most exciting incident in these chapters.

5 Compare and contrast Sikes and Fagin in these chapters.

6 Show how Dickens creates a particular atmosphere either in Chapter 19 or Chapter 20.

Chapter 21

The description of the journey out of London, with Sikes dragging Oliver after him. They get a lift in a cart most of the way; then they walk on and on until they pass Sunbury Church, and reach – near some water that scares Oliver – a lonely and dilapidated house.

Commentary

Note the creation of atmosphere and once again the meticulous attention to detail on the journey. There is a splendid sense of the city and, more particularly, the market, and of their effect upon Oliver. There is a great feeling of haste, too, which matches the narrative tension. The cunning of Sikes in getting a lift is evident. Atmosphere, consonant with Oliver's fear, builds up as he thinks Sikes has brought him to this lonely place to murder him.

Sun Street... into Smithfield One of the features of *Oliver Twist* (indeed of most of Dickens's novels) is the extraordinarily detailed knowledge shown of London and its environs – perhaps drawn from the novelist's memories of his long night walks in the city.
drovers i.e. drivers of flocks, cattle-dealers.
take a morning dram i.e. a small draught of spirits.
to bear him up To give him courage.
There was a dull sound of falling water... It seemed like quiet music for the repose of the dead Every now and then in Dickens there is a kind of poetic writing, used as a contrast with what has gone before.

Chapter 22

In the house they find Barney (the waiter in the public house at Saffron Hill) and Flash Toby Crackit, who is described. They eat and drink (Oliver is forced to do so by Sikes); then all the equipment for the burglary is produced. By now it is dark and they set off for Chertsey. Oliver begs to be released, but Sikes gets him to the house and manages to force him through the aperture. The result is that Oliver advances stealthily, is shot at from the head of the stairs and wounded; then Sikes fires his pistol at the servants and escapes with Oliver.

Commentary

Crackit is another in the line of eccentrics, but the main interest here is in the continuing atmosphere of tension. The equipment is described, with slang terms appropriate to the burglars' vocabulary. The high drama comes with Oliver's begging to be let go, followed by Sikes's menacing of him and Toby Crackit's good sense in not letting Sikes fire at him (Oliver). This is succeeded by more drama as Oliver is shot, but we note that Sikes, albeit fleetingly, shows compassion for the boy.

as if you took laudanum with your meals This is tincture of opium: ironically mentioned here, since later on Nancy is to drug Sikes with laudanum so that she can keep her assignation with Rose Maylie and Mr Brownlow on London Bridge.
cub id Come in.
wenture Venture.

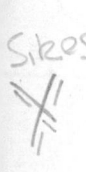

Wud of One of.
His mug is a fortun His face is an asset. (Oliver always looks innocent).
younker Youngster.
to the crack To the housebreaking.
A drain for the boy i.e. a drink for Oliver.
perwerse Perverse, awkward, obstinate.
Barkers Pistols.
The persuaders Weapons.
darkies Lanterns with a sliding shutter to keep the light hidden until it is to be used.
Slap through the town Straight through the town.
He's game enough i.e. brave enough.
limb Mischievous child.
'ticed i.e. enticed, lured.
the sensation of being carried over uneven ground at a rapid pace Note how the narrative suddenly switches into Oliver's consciousness, in order to convey the immediacy of what is happening.

Chapter 23

Now there is a complete transfer of attention, and we find ourselves with Bumble, on a bitterly cold night, visiting Mrs Corney. The preamble of courtship is described, with the beadle taking a cup of reinforced tea and delighting in the domestic cosiness engendered by the presence of Mrs Corney's cats. Just as Bumble is about to broach the subject of matrimony, Mrs Corney is informed that a pauper by the name of Old Sally is about to die. When she has gone to investigate this, Bumble inspects the teaspoons and other portable articles in order to assess the value of Mrs Corney's holdings before finally committing himself.

Commentary

Note the immediate contrast which, in a sense, is disconcerting, since we as readers are keyed up to know what happens to Oliver. The author's concern for the 'hunger-worn outcasts' is compassionate, but the comedy between Mrs Corney and Mr Bumble is dominated by self-interest, with each intent on his/her own thoughts and the deception of the other. Callousness towards the paupers is evident in both of them, Bumble ingratiates himself with Mrs Corney (the height of the ridiculous is his calling an ungrateful cat an 'ass'), and the dramatic interruption is, of course, an important element in the unravelling of the plot.

The night was bitter cold. The snow lay on the ground There is an echo of Keats's *Eve of St Agnes* here, but Bumble hardly resembles young Porphyro 'on fire' for Madeline.
Anti-porochial i.e. against the parish, a ridiculous sense of perspective.
a copper farthing's worth i.e. not worth anything, a farthing being the smallest coin before the advent of decimilization, one-quarter of a penny.
as brazen as alabaster The simile indicates the limited range of Bumble's imagination.
and he *did* in the streets Dickens never allows us to forget the terrible reality – here made all the more ironic in the mouth of Bumble.
***so* happy, *so* frolicsome, and *so* cheerful** Their state may be contrasted with that of the paupers, and further underlines the point made above.
and danced with much gravity four distinct times round the table Dickens is always ready with the grotesque, but once again we are aware of the theatrical nature of this, for it is made all the more ridiculous by the fact of being done in mime.

Chapter 24

A very short chapter, with the apothecary's apprentice in attendance, expecting the death of his patient in the next couple of hours. The two old hags who are watching recall old Sally's watching in her time. But they are turned out at the express order of the dying woman, who wants to say something to Mrs Corney. She reveals that she took a locket from Oliver's mother.

Commentary

An author comment on the appearance of death before we come to the specific death of old Sally. Before that, there is the sordid and degrading exchange between the two old women, the unconcern of Mrs Corney, and the dramatic incident of old Sally rising in her bed. Sally's is the death-bed confession essential to the plot, mysterious to us but arousing expectation about Oliver's origins.

It's all U.P. there Common emphasis, meaning 'it's all up'; there is no hope.
harridans Haggard old women, vixens.
The gold I stole was— Typical Dickensian technique of keeping the mystery going, setting up suspense in the reader's mind.

Chapter 25

Again the point of the narration is moved. Fagin is in the old den with the Dodger, Charley Bates and Tom Chitling, the three last named playing whist. The Dodger is systematically robbing Chitling who, we learn, is in love with Betsy, and who thus has to suffer a degree of ridicule on this account. They are interrupted by the arrival of an anything-but-flash Toby Crackit. Fagin rushes out of the house when he hears that Oliver has been hit and that there is no news of the whereabouts of Sikes.

Commentary

This narrative switch maintains dramatic tension, since we still don't know what has happened to Oliver (and Sikes). The Dodger is a cheat, very cunning, while Charley Bates is impetuous; the card-game reveals the Dodger's manifestly superior intelligence. Chitling is a dupe, and Charley's sophisticated sense of humour at times gets the better of him and causes him to choke and roll about. Fagin is a great fretter and worrier, here certainly with cause, but there is a kind of black comedy in the way Toby Crackit delays his account of what has happened at Chertsey. The irony is that he doesn't know what has happened to Sikes, for he expected that he would be with Fagin.

peculiarly intelligent This quality is stressed in the Dodger, and adds to the sense of loss we feel at his being reduced to crime.
a scientific rubber i.e. a carefully calculated and worked out game of whist.
two doubles and the rub Two tricks (in cards) and the best of three games.
you must get up very early in the morning i.e. you must be very fresh and sharp.
to cut any gentleman ... at a shilling a time i.e. the first one to draw or cut a picture card wins the money.
a ground-plan of Newgate Presumably in case he is ever sent there. Perhaps he is working out how to escape.
a merry-go-rounder Here's a surprise!
spree A lively frolic, bout of drinking.
milled Jailed.
if I'd split upon her i.e. if I had informed against her.
castor Hat.
when I cut i.e. when I make a run for it.

48 Oliver Twist

afore the old file now i.e. before the old cunning ones.
Day and Martin The liquid blacking made by Day and Martin.
a bubble of blacking Not even a drop of blacking.
fill-out i.e. a good meal.

Chapter 26

Fagin goes off towards Field Lane, meets Mr Lively on the way, then heads for the Three Cripples. Fagin joins the company there, and here we have a vivid description of the mixed criminals, male and female. There is no news of Barney, but Monks is expected to arrive. Fagin decides to double-back and go to Sikes's 'residence' in order to discover if Nancy knows anything. He finds Nancy incapable (either drunk or upset), and he is so incensed by her attitude that he nearly gives away what he himself knows has happened to Oliver. Nancy hopes that Oliver is dead (so she says) and her conscience is obviously troubling her. She smells strongly of gin, however, and Fagin concludes that she has not really understood what he has been talking about. He goes off, and on reaching the corner of his own street, meets Monks. The two repair to Fagin's den where Monks reprimands Fagin for not doing with Oliver what he has said he would (little does he know the truth!). Monks's nerves temporarily desert him when he glimpses the shadow of a woman passing by. They look in all the rooms but are unable to locate the mysterious figure. Fagin confirms that the outer door was locked.

Commentary

The chapter generates excitement, beginning with Fagin nearly being run down, and goes on to portray the sordid existence of criminals. The interior of the Three Cripples is particularly squalid, though there is a distinct atmosphere, what we should call a 'pub' atmosphere, with the woman singing and the description of the various types present. Fagin's conversation with the landlord shows how corrupt he is, and his words with Nancy indicate that he is intent on getting Sikes hanged if Oliver is not returned to him. He realizes that he has almost given away the game to Nancy, who manages to keep up her act of being either drunk or partly drugged into stupidity. The conversation between Monks and Fagin shows the former intent on the corruption of Oliver but not on his death, which he fears would haunt him. The outline of the woman is a fine dramatic stroke.

denizens Inhabitants, occupants.
It was curious to observe some faces Study this paragraph closely for a clear indication of Dickens's capacity for *observation* – this is a superb visual representation of a sordid cross-section of life at the time.
I'll pound it i.e. I'll bet.
Let him alone for that You can trust him to be able to do that.
Jack Ketch He was the notorious executioner of Charles II's reign, his name becoming a synonym for all who followed him in that office. He is thought to have beheaded the Duke of Monmouth in 1685.
I could whistle away i.e. easily betray.
You put me up for a minute i.e. raised my spirits.
perfume of Geneva i.e. of the spirits (she had been drinking).
the justice of the Jew's supposition The accuracy of his guess.
colloquy Conversation.

Chapter 27

Another narrative switch – this time presumably to increase tension and anticipation – back to Bumble and Mrs Corney. Bumble proposes marriage, and we learn that the post of workhouse master will shortly fall vacant. After he has been accepted by the coy Corney, Bumble steps out into the cold air and goes to Sowerberry to tell him of the death of old Sally. Arrived there, he finds the gluttonous Noah being indulged with oysters by Charlotte. Bumble, as we should expect, castigates Noah for attempting to kiss Charlotte, an ironic attitude in view of the fact that he himself had been kissing Mrs Corney not a few minutes previously.

Commentary

The main plot and the comic plot, later connected, continue to hold the balance of the narrative. The opening paragraph adopts a mock-heroic tone towards the courtship of the amorous beadle, always with an eye on the latter's financial weighing-up of the advantages of matrimony with Mrs Corney. After the affectation of being overcome, soon restored by spirits, Mrs Corney actively encourages Bumble as he moves towards the proposal through a series of calculations, even to the death of the workhouse master, which would provide 'a joining of hearts and housekeepings'. Oysters put Noah in an amorous mood and he attempts to kiss Charlotte. She, however, is much braver than he is when confronted by the righteously indignant – and hypocritical – Bumble.

the divine right of beadles An ironic use of the phrase normally applied to kings – and more particularly the Bourbon and Stuart dynasties, who asserted that their power came from the Almighty.
such a pleasant dog His attitude is certainly 'waggish' or humorous.
placed the other over her heart, and gasped for breath Mrs Corney is acting, and here the appearance/reality theme is evident: she thinks this is the best way to win Bumble.
I couldn't, – oh! The top shelf in the right hand corner The comedy lies in the hypocrisy of the lady, but it bodes ill for Bumble – for she is capable of a devastatingly sharp change of mind. We are reminded of Julia in Byron's *Don Juan*: 'And saying she would ne'er consent – consented.'
Coals, candles, and house-rent free Another emphasis on the economics rather than the romance of love.
my fascinator Bumble waxing poetic – he caps it with the more prosaic 'a joining of hearts and housekeepings'.
When is it to come off? i.e. when shall we be married?
a old woman's shell A coffin.

Chapter 28

Yet another movement of narration, for Sikes is forced to leave Oliver, largely through the cowardice of Toby Crackit. Three men, two of whom are Mr Giles and Brittles, are giving reluctant chase; the third is the travelling tinker. They are all agreed not to continue with the pursuit. Oliver is left senseless, his arm roughly bandaged in a shawl. Weak from loss of blood, he staggers on until he comes to a house that he thinks he recognizes. Meanwhile the three men concerned are sitting in the kitchen recounting the night's events when they hear a knock at the door. They are loath to open it, but when they finally do so they see poor Oliver. Rose Maylie appears, but returns upstairs, and on her instructions Giles carries Oliver upstairs 'with the care and solicitude of a woman'.

Commentary

Sikes shows his courage, Crackit his cowardice, and there is a comic element in the half-heartedness of the pursuit. Brittles and Giles are almost a comic act of their own, while the author's commentary on their simultaneously experiencing the same feelings, adds another dimension to the comedy. Oliver's delirium is superbly portrayed but there is pathos too, and apprehension, as Oliver nears the house. Inside, the comedy continues as Giles delights in describing the strange noise that woke him but is suitably startled when knocking is heard at the door. The loud talk to give the false impression that there are a number of men present is comic too but Rose Maylie's instructions move Giles from complacency and boastfulness to compassion and solicitude. Although we have only just met her, we realize that Rose is a symbol of goodness.

were recruiting themselves i.e. building up their strength by eating and drinking.
Of *shoes*, sir Another aspect of Dickens's comedy – again there is a flavour of the music-hall and the timed act of the comedian.
a master-stroke of policy Clever strategy.
as if he was a-going i.e. dying – a reference to Oliver's pallor.

Chapter 29

There is a description of Rose and Mrs Maylie and of their care and concern for Oliver. Their doctor friend Losberne arrives, rallies Giles on his shooting ability, and attends to Oliver. At this stage the ladies don't realize – not having seen him – that the thief is a child.

Commentary

The description of the two ladies is idealized and overly sentimental in the case of Rose, though she does make a joke in terms of Brittles still being a boy. Losberne shows himself to be a man of wit and spirit, with a genuine concern for the ladies. There is some humour in Giles's having received much praise, though he has only shot a boy – quite naturally, he wants to retain some glory for what he has done. Losberne loves the mystery of the ladies being in ignorance of the 'criminal's' age.

a waiter A tray.
in the little offices of the table i.e. eating and drinking, buttering toast etc.

to hit your man at twelve paces The phrase smacks of duelling practice.

Chapter 30

Losberne takes the ladies into the room where Oliver is lying. There follows a description of Oliver and the reactions of the ladies at the sight of him. They are all convinced of his innocence, and the doctor says that he will bully Giles and Brittles so that their version of what happened is changed, thus making it impossible for the police to charge Oliver. Losberne sets to work, but just as he has made Giles and Brittles uncertain in their identification of Oliver, the Bow Street runners arrive: Brittles, in an excess of efficiency, has sent for them.

Commentary

Unashamedly sentimental, with Rose revealing her kindness of heart and faith in the goodness of human nature. Losberne is rational – and underneath it kind – and his bullying of Giles and Brittles a masterpiece of deception in the best interests of Oliver and those who care for him.

to regale himself To eat and drink freely.

Revision questions on Chapters 21–30

1 Give an account of the attempted burglary at Chertsey, explaining exactly what went wrong.

2 Bring out the nature of the comedy in the two scenes involving Mr Bumble and Mrs Corney in these chapters.

3 Indicate Dickens's capacity to increase narrative tension at the end of any *two* chapters in this sequence.

4 What do you consider the most exciting incident in these chapters and why? Give a detailed account of it.

5 Describe the characters of *either* Brittles and Giles *or* Losberne and Rose Maylie.

Chapter 31

Blathers and Duff, and their methods of going about their investigation, are described: this is followed by their interrogation of the two servants; then their own consultation, theories and reminiscences with each other. Meanwhile, the doctor discusses the situation with Rose. When Blathers and Duff reappear they are still caught up in their own theories, and engage in an elaborate recital of the deeds of one Conkey Chickweed, who plays a major part in their criminal mythology. Blathers and Duff eventually see Oliver; Giles is humiliated by his failure to be positive in his identification; Brittles indulges in a mass of contradictions; Blathers and Duff do not solve the case (Conkey Chickweed bulks large in their reasoning), but receive a small financial consideration in return for their negative capabilities.

Commentary

Blathers and Duff are pedantic, heavy-handed, obvious – a Dickensian parody of police officers. Losberne's goodness of heart is evident in his trying to cover up for Oliver. The story of Conkey Chickweed is funny, but it is used to expose Blathers as a time-waster. Losberne easily fools the two men over the pistol, Giles's contradictions and the gullibility of the two officers further help to establish Oliver's 'innocence', and the author waxes ironic about 'the English law, and its comprehensive love of all the king's subjects'. The chapter ends sentimentally with the care of Oliver by Rose, Mrs Maylie and Mr Losberne.

the prad The horse.
coach-'us Coach-house.
several muscular affections i.e. twisting and turning himself about.
a yokel A simple country fellow.
a pair of castanets Hardwood or ivory instruments used in pairs to rattle in time with dancing.
a consultation of great doctors on the knottiest points in medicine, would be mere child's play A superb piece of irony to underline the pompous self-importance of Blathers and Duff – an irony further extended when you think that human life is involved in their deliberations too.
badger-drawing i.e. setting dogs to draw badgers from casks.
blunderbuss Ancient short gun with large bore firing many balls.

blunt Money.
licensed witler Licensed victualler, a publican.
a active officer A detective, but not in uniform.
spring-gun i.e. a gun which goes off when a trespasser or an animal stumbles into it.

Chapter 32

Oliver recovers, and is of course grateful to Rose Maylie. With the doctor they set out to trace Mr Brownlow. When they get to Chertsey, where Oliver had stayed with Sikes and Toby Crackit, they are greeted by an indignant hunchback who naturally denies any knowledge of the two housebreakers. Later they discover that Mr Brownlow has gone away, and Oliver is sent into the country to recuperate. In three months he becomes 'completely domesticated with the old lady and her niece'.

Commentary

This is an excessively sentimental chapter. The dialogue between Rose and Oliver sounds contrived. The encounter with the hunchback raises tension, as does the visit to Mr Brownlow's, but this is soon subsumed in Oliver's peaceful – and idealized – life in the country. We are away from the area of realism which Dickens knows so well, and the result is a partial failure of the imagination.

a chariot and pair i.e. a coach with two horses harnessed together.
to bait the horses i.e. to feed them.
cupidity Greed.
would be a-foot i.e. up and about.
a thousand commendations Lavish praises. Note the tone: the unreal nature of the presentation of Rose Maylie and Oliver is largely accounted for by stylistic excesses such as this one.

Chapter 33

A high-temperature point in the narrative, for Rose Maylie is suddenly taken ill and her life is in danger. Oliver is despatched to send a letter to Harry Maylie, but on his way to do so he encounters a stranger who, when he sees him, falls down and writhes in a fit. Next morning the beauty and joy of the landscape are contrasted with Rose's state, but later in the day Doctor

Losberne assures Mrs Maylie and Oliver that Rose will live. Perhaps one ought to say that the autobiographical circumstances that led to this chapter's being included in *Oliver Twist* are well known (the death of Dickens's beloved sister-in-law), but the chapter serves the plot in only one way: it reveals to Oliver the existence of Monks (though Oliver doesn't know who he is).

Commentary

The illness of Rose Maylie and its factual basis have been referred to above. The dialogue is marred by sentiment, exaggeration and an unsuccessful attempt to create an atmosphere of doubt. Even the meeting with the unidentified Monks is melodramatic in the extreme and Oliver's chancing upon a funeral service while waiting for news of Rose, is too obvious a symbol of his suffering. The coming contrast is obvious – the end of the chapter is not a cliffhanger but a final assertion of the goodness of God in a world which exists apart from the world of Sikes, Fagin, Bumble, Mrs Corney, and even Monks.

Spring flew swiftly by The first three paragraphs are redolent of natural description which contrasts with what is to come; the prose, the quality of the description, are undistinguished.

she gave Oliver her purse, and he started off We are reminded forcibly of Oliver's other errand, for Mr Brownlow, and what happened to him. This duplication within the plot has the effect of raising narrative tension.

ostler A stableman at the inn.

Curses light upon your head, and black death upon your heart, you imp! Note the melodramatic tone – but it is stagey and again undermines the realistic quality.

Chapter 34

Happiness is complete with Rose's recovery, and Giles and Harry Maylie arrive to contribute additional joy. Harry is delighted to learn that Rose is better, and he confides to his mother that he intends to propose to Rose later. Losberne continues to tease Giles. Oliver, working at his lessons one day, falls asleep, but is aware of a man (and Fagin) looking in upon him; he cries out when he wakes fully.

Commentary

Oliver and Harry are greatly moved by Rose's recovery, and we must not overlook the relief of Giles. Mrs Maylie is practical when reprimanded by her son for not writing, and sensitive on the question of Rose's own sensitivity about her 'doubtful birth', so much so that she counsels the impetuous Harry to be cautious in approaching her. Giles's reward provides downstairs conversational fuel. The effect on Oliver of his recognition of Fagin and Monks is underlined by the constricting atmosphere that descends once the Jew reappears in the narrative.

The birds were once more hung out, to sing, in their old places With the recovery of Rose in the idyllic country setting Dickens indulges in the sentimental harmony, a little overdone, of nature and the patient.

Chapter 35

Harry, Giles and Losberne search for Fagin and Monks, but without success. Rose recovers and Harry proposes to her, but she rejects him on the grounds that her lack of birth would be an encumbrance to him in public life. But he gets permission to speak to her again on the subject.

Commentary

The excitement of the search, which yields nothing, and occasional humour from Losberne is all that relieves the sentiment of this chapter. Harry proposes at great length and with much emotion, and Rose weeps in turn at having to reject him. The dialogue is maudlin and mawkish.

mingling with the spent and feeble stream of life Harry is too given to the imagery of nature, which makes for romance but not for reality.
it will shed a gleam of happiness upon my lonely way The preceding comment also applies here.

Chapter 36

Harry Maylie departs for public life, but asks Oliver to write to him once a fortnight, to give him news of his mother and of Rose. Rose sheds secret tears at Harry's departure.

Commentary

A linking chapter, with Oliver honoured by his commission and Losberne the only flesh and blood human being in these exchanges.

great nobs i.e. important, influential people.
place, cup, or sweepstakes All references to horse-racing.
your felicitious illustration i.e. the happy example (you have chosen).
postillion The rider of the near horse of the leaders.

Chapter 37

We return to a gloomy Mr Bumble, reduced after two months of marriage, to complete subservience to the ex-Mrs Corney. The confrontation between them is described, with Mrs Bumble physically victorious over Bumble, who is tumbled over a chair on to the floor. Afterwards he goes to the wash-house; but his wife is there and humiliates him further. He makes his retreat, and goes to a pub. There he encounters a stranger who reveals that he has been looking for him. He asks Bumble to recall the birth of Oliver in the workhouse and the part played by old Sally. Bumble reveals that he knows who was with old Sally at her death; and the stranger reveals in turn that his name is Monks.

Commentary

Bumble has got his just deserts – the bully is reduced to the coward that he is. Both he and Mrs Corney deserve each other. Dickens employs much rhetoric to demonstrate that Bumble, like other 'great' men, is only a man. The battle is a strategic one which Mrs Bumble wins because she is stronger, more intelligent, and clever. There is a slapstick and grotesque humour about the scene and the humiliation. This is compounded when Bumble insensitively encroaches upon the matron's rights in the washroom. Monks knows his man once he begins to talk to Bumble, for he has seen before that the beadle is motivated by greed. The latter motive induces Bumble to promise Monks more information, as he possesses low cunning enough to try to play Monks at his own game.

counsellor An advising barrister.
the small one-pair The room at the top of a flight of stairs.
a porochial bye-word i.e. everyone would hold me up as an example (of being ruled by my wife).
be in the way i.e. might (not) be here.
height and pomp of beadleship, to the lowest depth of the most snubbed henpeckery A superb use of antithesis to indicate Bumble's changed state and status.
reversing the axiom i.e. changing the word order and therefore the sense of the proverbial saying.
jorum A large drinking bowl, usually containing punch.
sovereigns British gold coins worth nominally £1 each.
lying-in room Room set aside for childbearing women in labour.
murrain A plague (infectious disease in cattle).
tirade Loud condemnation.
no midwifery there i.e. where she's gone (meaning that she's dead).

Chapter 38

Mr and Mrs Bumble keep their assignation with Monks – the beadle sorely apprehensive, his wife unafraid. Monks agrees to pay twenty-five guineas in gold for the information that Mrs Bumble will reveal. Mrs Bumble tells how she took a pawn ticket from old Sally on the night of her death and how she redeemed what was pawned. This she hands over to Monks: the gold locket, two locks of hair, and a plain gold wedding ring. The three people are standing where there had once been a watermill, and Monks destroys this evidence by throwing it into the swollen waters. After that they leave, pledged to secrecy.

Commentary

Fine sense of dramatic atmosphere from the beginning of the chapter, with the dilapidated building symbolic of the decadent criminals. Mrs Bumble is well in control. Monks, however, is affected by the lightning and thunder, which are manifestations of Hell to him, explaining away his distorted and discoloured face as a tendency to fits. There is something comic in Bumble's teeth-chattering bravado, quickly silenced by his wife's bluntness. Note how she tells the story of old Sally explicitly and directly, thus creating in Monks a corresponding excitement. It is good narrative, essential to the plot, though Dickens still maintains the mystery.

trained down i.e. reduced (Bumble could only take on someone much weaker than himself.)
It fell straight, and true as a die; clove the water with a scarcely audible splash; and was gone A fine example of the superb graphic economy of description that Dickens often achieves: in telling contrast to his high-flown and sentimental indulgences.

Chapter 39

Now we are taken back to Sikes: he has been nursed through a fever by Nancy after the Chertsey expedition. Nancy is exhausted and hysterical when Fagin, the Dodger and Charley Bates arrive. They restore Nancy, and give Sikes plenty of food and drink, which they've brought with them. We learn that Sikes has been left in this state, as he puts it, for three weeks; and in spite of the food he is very abusive to Fagin who, after a long wrangle, agrees to allow Sikes some money. Nancy goes back with Fagin and the boys, and Toby Crackit is there when they arrive. He has been swindling the ever-gullible Chitling at cards. The boys set off for 'work' and Fagin goes to get Nancy the cash for Sikes. But Monks arrives and goes upstairs with Fagin; Nancy is very pale when they return. She goes back to Sikes, but next day becomes very excited. Sikes believes that she is getting the fever but, when he is asleep, Nancy sneaks out and goes to call on Rose Maylie at her hotel. The latter agrees to see her.

Commentary

Nancy's suffering is highlighted through her devoted nursing of Sikes. The strain is shown in her fainting, her comparing of Sikes to 'a child' reflecting her obsession with Oliver. Charley Bates proves once again his capacity for enjoyment, whether he is ministering to Nancy or praising the food they have brought for Sikes. Fagin shows his meanness and his bargaining powers, Chitling his easy stupidity, Nancy her capacity for deception in what we suspect is her concern for Oliver. We particularly note her observation of Monks, but after her eavesdropping on Fagin and Monks no acting can eliminate her pallor, caused presumably by what she has heard. She has the spirit and the ingenuity to drug Sikes with laudanum, but such is her feeling for the robber that she kisses him on her way out. Her courage is never in question as she fights to see Rose, and the chapter ends on a note of Dickensian irony at the expense of the four respectable chambermaids who describe Nancy as 'shameful'.

don't come over me Don't try to impose on me or trick me.
encomiums Praises.
sitch delicate creeturs i.e. such tender creatures.
half a pound of seven and sixpenny green i.e. tea.
Two half-quartern brans Two 2lb loaves.
pound of best fresh i.e. butter.
the richest sort you've ever lushed i.e. wine you've ever drunk.
drayma Drama.
withered old fence A reference to Fagin's thinness and meanness at the same time.
mull Mess.
wiper Thief.
I'll pound it I'll bet.
perwented Prevented.
taking leave of his affectionate friend Note the heavy irony here, for Fagin and Sikes hate each other.
Not a living leg i.e. no one.
as dull as swipes i.e. as flat beer.
as fast as Newgate That could be sounder than the last sleep of Newgate – the sleep of death.
at fifteen sixpences an interview i.e. his losses at cards.
heavy swell I suppose that we should say 'really with it'.
on the lay On the lookout.
spirited young bloods i.e. reckless young men of fashion.
stauncher-hearted gal i.e. loyal and true.
A watchman was crying half-past-nine A reference to the practice of calling the time through the streets.
a few made head upon her i.e. overtook her.
Brass can do better than the gold what has stood the fire i.e. what is inferior is likely to achieve more than what is rare. The reference is to Nancy's 'profession' by those who would consider themselves 'respectable'. Dickens's own irony on their account is shown by his referring to them as 'Dianas' – Diana was the goddess of hunting and of chastity.

Chapter 40

This is Nancy's interview with Rose, in which she confesses her part in the attempted corruption of Oliver. She also tells of Monks, and his role in the continued criminal activity. And when she leaves she arranges to walk on London Bridge every Sunday evening between 11 and 12.

Commentary

Rose's kindness moves Nancy, but the latter's revelations are important to the working out of the plot. There is a considered stress on Nancy's loyalty to her kind, despite her knowledge of their evil. Of particular focus and force is her expressed loyalty to Sikes. Nancy's feelings are probed to their very depths.

the stews Brothels.
hulks Bodies of dismantled ships used as prisons.

Revision questions on Chapters 31–40

1 Indicate the part played in the investigation by Blathers and Duff.

2 In what ways does the illness of Rose Maylie influence the course of events in these chapters?

3 Give some account of the character of Harry Maylie.

4 Describe the roles played by Mr and Mrs Bumble in these chapters.

5 Describe the events which lead to Nancy's interview with Rose Maylie.

Chapter 41

Rose is making up her mind what to do, when Oliver comes to her with the news that he has just seen Mr Brownlow. Rose immediately goes to see him and finds him with Mr Grimwig. She reveals that Oliver is with her, and receives as a reward a kiss from Mr Grimwig. Mrs Bedwin too arrives to join in the celebration, exclaiming 'my innocent boy' when she sees Oliver. Losberne is also told of Nancy's visit, but after discussion with Brownlow they all agree to keep Nancy's secret and to try to discover the true story of Oliver's parentage. Mrs Maylie decides that she and Rose will stay in town until the mystery is solved.

Commentary

Rose shows some character in determining to keep Nancy's revelations secret for the moment, while narrative tension is built up by Oliver's seeing Mr Brownlow. Rose's visit to him is marked by the eccentricity of Mr Grimwig and the latter's delight just to prove, as if we didn't know it, that beneath that tough exterior he has a heart of gold. Losberne's reaction to the story of Nancy is impetuous and irrational, Brownlow's a more balanced one. The adding of Harry Maylie to the committee brings him within Rose's romantic orbit again, and we note with interest that Mr Brownlow too has a secret which he will reveal at a later date.

some ventriloquial power Again, the influence of the music-hall is apparent here.
lightsome Graceful, elegant, nimble.
a very Quixotic act A reference to Don Quixote, the hero of Cervantes' episodic novel of that name, who constantly undertook deeds of honour and devotion regardless of material cost to himself.

Chapter 42

This is another switch in the narrative, for we see Noah Claypole and Charlotte advancing towards London prior to becoming embroiled in the main plot again. Charlotte, of course, is carrying the luggage. They arrive at the Three Cripples and are greeted by Barney when they ask for a room and something to eat. Fagin is there, overhears Noah's criminal ambitions, and makes himself known to the young couple. Fagin 'cons' twenty pounds out of Noah to pay for his 'training' and decides to start Noah off on the 'kinchin lay' – stealing from small children. Noah becomes 'Morris Bolter'.

Commentary

Noah Claypole in recognizable bullying form making Charlotte do all the heavy work, Charlotte as subservient as ever. Noah thinks he has the brains, ironically of course he is shortly to reveal his gullibility. Nonetheless, he has had the low cunning to let Charlotte carry the money so that she will be blamed if they are apprehended. Barney and Fagin obviously work together, and Fagin's repetition of Noah's remarks gives that young man an uncomfortable moment, a moment which reveals his cowardice as he tries to blame Charlotte for his own words. Claypole is despicable, Charlotte silly, Fagin well in control before his own fall.

the dabe of this ouse The name . . .
I'b dot certaid you cad I'm not certain you can.
homeopathic Strictly for the treatment of a disease, but here the treatment consists of food and drink.
ridicules Noah means 'reticules' (bags), the only time he displays a Dodger-like propensity for misusage; but Noah's is ignorance, the Dodger's inspired distortion.
whopping of 'em i.e. the beating of them.
You've hit the right nail upon the head i.e. you have come to the right place and the right people.
a power of hands A number of assistants.
town-maders i.e. London-made or Londoners.
something very light i.e. not involving much physical effort.
A little fancy work? Fagin is probably being ironic, for he has summed up Noah's limitations. It means living off the proceeds of prostitution.
a few good beats chalked out i.e. areas where you could operate.

Chapter 43

Fagin instructs Noah the next day, but the disconcerting news is the arrest of the Dodger; Fagin and the boys pay their verbal tributes to him, and Fagin promises that he will be looked after (get what he wants) in prison. They speculate on the Dodger's coming court performance, and it is decided that Bolter will go to the police office to see what happens. The dock and the court at large are described; and the Dodger's rhetorical tirade, his consummate mishandling of the English language, is one of the comic high-spots of the novel. But he is taken away and committed for trial.

Commentary

The play on 'number one' indicates Fagin's cunning and his self-insurance in terms of blackmail. There is a certain cunning on the author's part, too, in making this conversation between Fagin and Noah lead naturally to the Dodger, and Charley Bates, even on this sad occasion, has recourse to humour. This gives way to sadness on account of the fact that the Dodger's honour and glory are not widely enough known, that he may not even figure in the Newgate Calendar. Fagin has sufficient imagination to anticipate what the Dodger will make of a court scene. The Dodger's scene is one of the funniest in the novel; he has verve, employs, or rather deploys, his malapropisms to good effect, and of course loses. Adhering to the scene is a terrible pathos, the criminality of a boy who has become a man before his time.

number one Fagin's definition is important, not merely because Noah is ignorant but because Fagin himself, while ensuring his own importance to those he employs, would in fact give them away (witness his attitude towards Sikes) and is thus more corrupt than they are.
the cravat . . . the halter i.e. the hangman's noose.
finger-post i.e. which gives directions at the parting of the roads.
lagging . . . lifer Later translated as 'transportation for life'.
lummy First-rate.
sneeze-box i.e. snuff-box.
top-sawyer First class.
it isn't on the rec-ord . . . come out in the 'dictment Charley is bemoaning the fact that the Dodger's best work will never be known because he got away with it! His pride in his friend makes him wish that all his achievements could be referred to, so that everybody in court would know what a brilliant criminal he was.
big-wig . . . gift of the gab A prominent defending counsel who is a fluent speaker.
the chief actor in a scene of most uncommon and exquisite humour And of course, Charley is right, as the event proves, and again the appearance (acting) covers the reality (guilt).
cutting away . . . wittles i.e. running away . . . food.
sitivation Situation.
and pepper with 'em i.e. something to make you hot (a prison sentence).
beaks Judges.
old files i.e. cunning men.
deformation Defamation. (One is reminded of the Dogberry scenes in Shakespeare's *Much Ado About Nothing*, where there is a play on the word 'deformed'.)
abase . . . descending The Dodger is, so to speak, in full flood. Here he means 'debase' and 'condescending'.
redress Address.
the shop i.e. the place.
Wice President Of course there isn't one: a pathetic instance of the Dodger's ignorance and of his bravado.

Chapter 44

Nancy's feelings, and her bitterness towards Fagin are described. It is Sunday, and Nancy wants to go out to keep her appointment, but she becomes hysterical when restrained by

Sikes. She shows Fagin out, who offers her freedom in return for betraying Sikes.

Commentary

Nancy often near hysteria or breakdown, and a fine dramatic and moving scene when Sikes restrains her. There is also a terrible moment when Fagin almost touches Nancy and we feel her physical repulsion. Notice that Fagin's conclusions are wrong, but his opportunist attempt to use Nancy against Sikes has an accompanying irony – Nancy is already working against *him* and, inadvertently, against Sikes.

you jade Woman (but here with a curse).
on the other tack i.e. becoming hysterical.
myrmidons Hired ruffians, based on the warlike Thessalians who followed Achilles.

Chapter 45

Fagin busy buttering up Noah Claypole in order to get him to follow Nancy.

Commentary

Bolter's (Noah's) greed stressed, as well as his obvious humour. Fagin begins to realize what he has taken on in terms of expense with Noah, but succeeds in getting him to do what he wants. Narrative interest quickens as Noah follows Nancy.

betimes Before time, early.
dodge i.e. shadow, follow.
had . . . od Remember that it's Barney. This means 'hand' . . . 'on'.

Chapter 46

Nancy sets off for the appointment on London Bridge, followed by Bolter. Nancy has no knowledge of this, but is beset by an intuitive fear that something is wrong; her imagination is heightened. When they meet, she reveals to Brownlow that she has given Sikes laudanum in order to get away. In return Brownlow tells her that they propose to 'extort the secret' from

Monks; but Nancy refuses to betray Fagin and Sikes and go on to a new life. However, she does agree to put Monks into their hands, and gives an accurate physical description of him. Brownlow obviously recognizes Monks from her description – particularly the detail of the scald or burn. Brownlow further offers to take care of Nancy, who leaves them, watched by the unobserved listener, Noah Claypole.

Commentary

Considerable tension and fear aroused as Noah keeps Nancy in sight, even brushing against Mr Brownlow and Rose. She reveals her fears to them, the fact that she is obsessed by death, the references being almost an anticipation of her own. Note that Nancy's description of Monks and his habits causes Mr Brownlow to start. It is ironic that Nancy refuses to betray Sikes and Fagin in view of what happens to her. Tension runs the length of the chapter.

pilaster Rectangular column, especially one in a wall.
Mussulman Mohammedan.
Pharisee Self-righteous person, hypocrite.
beyond its pale i.e. beyond the reach of (hope).

Chapter 47

All Fagin's schemes are overturned by Noah's revelations. Fagin sends for Sikes, talks of betrayal, and then wakes Noah to confirm the story – especially down to the detail of Nancy's administering of laudanum to Sikes. Fagin tells Sikes to be crafty, but Sikes is too incensed to take heed. He returns, clubs Nancy with his pistol and, while she clasps Rose Maylie's handkerchief to the wound, he seizes a club and strikes her down.

Commentary

The most moving and violent episode in the novel, full of dramatic incidents, high feelings, culminating in the most terrible of all crimes, murder. First there is the account of Fagin's terrible passions as he contemplates his losses and the betrayal; his inward feelings communicate themselves quickly to the unsuspecting Sikes – ironic this, for Sikes has suspected Fagin in the past – and of course Noah's account is too much for him. All that is violent in Sikes comes to the surface. Fagin tells him to be cautious, but even here we feel that perhaps Fagin is calculating on getting rid of Sikes because he knows that he is bound to be too violent. The killing is too terrible to contemplate, though the rather obvious symbol of Rose Maylie's handkerchief comes between the reader and reality for a moment.

palter Haggle.
earwigged by the parson i.e. brought to confess by the chaplain (in gaol).

Chapter 48

Before the description of Sikes's flight there is a detailed account of the aftermath of the murder: Sikes's attempts to hide the body under a rug; his burning of the club; and his carrying of the dog to avoid spreading bloodstains. He sets off for the country, doubles back to London again, then goes to Hatfield. In a pub he listens to a man who says that he can remove stains and takes Sikes's hat in order to demonstrate. Sikes overturns the table and leaves quickly. He hears the coachman talking of the London murder, and then sets off towards St Albans. He tries to sleep in a shed, but is roused by shouts of 'fire'; he plays a frenzied part in the rescue, then decides to return to London. He attempts to drown Bulls-eye, but the dog will not come near enough to be tied up.

Commentary

A superb focus upon Sikes, the sun, his reaction to what he has done, his hysteria over the body. There is the terrible realism of the hair on the club which burns in the fire, while his journey, with its constantly turning back on itself, reflects the state of a mind which never can – what's done is done. The chapter is cunningly structured, the demonstration of the stain remover an ironic comment on the fact that nothing can remove the stain of murder. Sikes's hysterical reaction is in keeping with his guilt and the nature of his character, even his response to what he hears of the Spitalfields murder can be attributed to his vacillations of mood. His imagination is centered – his behaviour convincing, and even the nervous energy which drives him to try and rescue those in the fire is a reflex of his obsession. It is also, seen at another level, a subconscious wish to atone for his sin. The dog, the symbol of his guilt and of his brutality, cannot be removed, any more than the stain of the blood. The whole chapter is a superb piece of graphic writing.

mountebank A quack, a charlatan.
hones Whetstones, various stones for razors.
composition-cakes See following sentence in the text.
so's the young 'ooman of property A pleasant fancy that he is going to marry into money!

Chapter 49

Brownlow brings Monks to his house and Monks is forced into a series of revelations. He has to decide whether to confess or let Mr Brownlow prefer charges against him. Brownlow himself, in fact, reveals the details: that Monks (Edward Leeford) is Oliver's half-brother. Oliver's mother was loved by his father, and that father was in turn the great friend of Mr Brownlow. Monks agrees to make a full confession, and this means the coming indictment of Fagin. Meanwhile, there is every assurance that Sikes, too, will be taken.

Commentary

Here the plot gathers pace just as the narrative has gathered pace in the previous chapter. Coincidence is stretched, Brownlow gives a harrowing account of a marriage rooted in incompatability and reveals himself to have been quite a detective into the bargain. His rhetoric, the impressive and irrefutable nature of his findings, are too much for Monks – really Edward Leeford – and he is broken by the accusations. Losberne's entrance with the news of Sikes is also dramatic.

their heavy chain . . . clanking bond . . . galling fragment . . . rivets This comparison of a marriage to a kind of imprisonment links through the imagery with the coming imprisonment of Fagin.
vicious courses i.e. degrading behaviour or patterns of behaviour.
a hideous disease The symptoms appear to be those of an epileptic – in which case the description here of its origin does not fit.

Chapter 50

Jacob's Island, where we find Kags, Chitling and Toby Crackit together. They give the news that Fagin has been arrested, and that Betsy has gone mad after seeing the body of Nancy. Shortly after this the dog arrives, followed by Sikes; he gets a distant reception from his 'friends', and then Charley Bates turns up, throws himself on Sikes, and has to be pulled off. The mob surrounding the house begins an assault: Sikes makes for the roof-top, and takes a rope which he attaches to the stack – thinking to leap down and across the ditch to the prospect of safety. But he slips and accidentally hangs himself. Bulls-eye jumps from the parapet for his shoulders, misses, falls, and dashes out his brains.

Commentary

The graphic intensity continues. The sordid nature of the neighbourhood is underlined, the atmosphere of decay and filth indescribable, the whole a symbol for the degradation of people forced to live in such surroundings. Although the narrative is retrospective, at least in respect of Fagin and Bet, for instance, it is none the less effective. Particularly vivid is the arrest of Fagin with the mob trying to get at him. Even the appearance of the dog is a dramatic stroke which deludes the group temporarily, but the entrance of Charley Bates is masterly in its dramatic and moral effects. He is so changed from the humorous character we have known, that his sudden start into moral responsibility, while it may seem unlikely, is effective because of its intensity, particularly when he attacks Sikes. From then on the atmosphere is charged with excitement and imminent action, superb narrative art which culminates only with the death of Sikes and his dog. Note the economy, the visual force of the writing.

coal-whippers Coal heavers working on the docks.
raff As in riff-raff – presumably here, the dregs.
a returned transport i.e. one who had been transported for a crime but who had come back, risking the death penalty by so doing.
smelling about it i.e. estimating it, sizing it up.
strait-weskut i.e. a strait-jacket, so that she could not struggle and do herself or anybody an injury.
a smash This means ruin.
shrinking off i.e. their withdrawal from Sikes.

this screeching Hell-babe 'Turn, hell-hound, turn' says Macduff to Macbeth, and the whole of this sequence in *Oliver Twist* has echoes of Shakespeare's play – the eyes, the knocking, the blood – as well as this particular reference.

Chapter 51

Oliver is intent on going back to the farm to reclaim Dick, and on the way sees all the places he knew as a despised child. But he and Brownlow go to an hotel and Oliver meets his half-brother; shortly after, we learn of the burned will – if it had survived, his father's property would have been left half to Oliver and half to his mother. Now we learn that Rose is Oliver's aunt – but in his mind, of course, still his sister. Harry Maylie reveals that he has given up all thought of a public career and has become a clergyman. Meanwhile, Oliver's earliest friend, Dick, has died.

Commentary

Oliver comes alive in his enthusiasm – nothing has changed, but he now sees it all from a different perspective. The introduction of Monks is dramatic, with Oliver greatly moved by the story and the establishment of his identity. Fagin's role is fully explained as Monks's confidant with a special 'reward for keeping Oliver ensnared'. Bumble reveals the extent of his hypocrisy by his shameless attempt to ingratiate himself with Oliver and the company by saying how much he has missed him. He also shows how treacherous he can be by blaming everything on Mrs Bumble, and there is a grotesque moment when the two old crones are brought in to testify about the stealing of the locket and the rings. There is something arbitrary, idealistic, sentimental and totally unrealistic about Harry Maylie's decision. The chapter closes with Oliver's grief, a testimony to his loyal and affectionate memory.

palmed a tale i.e. misled somebody.
babbling drabs Talkative, degenerate old women.
the law is a ass – a idiot Again we are reminded of the language of Dogberry in *Much Ado About Nothing*.
the law is a bachelor i.e. is lacking experience.

Chapter 52

Fagin in court. He is found guilty and sentenced to death. His time in the cell is described; but though no reprieve is received, Oliver and Mr Brownlow come to see him. Fagin tells Oliver where the papers concerning him are hidden, and is then taken out to his death.

Commentary

This brief summary does scant justice to what for many is the finest chapter in the novel – a superb analysis of isolation, fear, degradation – the whole consequence of a life lived in corruption and self-seeking. The atmosphere is sustained throughout, so that if we are moved to pity for Fagin, it is the pity that wishes even this squalid wretch should not have to suffer the torture of waiting for death. Here we have that strange paradox of Dickens's writing, which can give both sides of a question, though it is clear where his own sympathies lie.

The focus on Fagin in the early part of the chapter is unremitting, but it gradually merges into the spectacle, terrible for him, yet almost casual for others, the spectators who have come to feast on the affair. Still they are seen from Fagin's heightened consciousness, thus giving us a sense of identification throughout. This does not diminish with the sentence; rather it is accentuated by Fagin's silence which is the outward mask for his inward tumult. The mark of compassion is shown in the mattress being brought in so that Fagin will not be alone; unlike Sikes, he wishes only for light. The passage of time is noted as superbly – and finally – as Sikes's journey in fear, for this is Fagin's last journey (of the imagination) to death. The past rears itself before him. His delirium rules him in a grotesque parody of what that past was. There is little doubt that he is mad at the end, and the end is spelled out by Dickens's description – nonetheless effective for being brief and humanitarian – of 'all the hideous apparatus of death'.

strong and vigorous men to dangling heaps of clothes Note the fine antithesis, almost as if the hanged man is a puppet – as indeed he is.
the real hours treading on each other's heels Note the unobtrusive but effective personification – every hour is *personal* to the man who awaits his death.
Good boy Charley ... Bolter's throat Fagin's mind is running on the

past, and of course on the fact that his latest protégé, Noah Claypole, has turned informer. Again there is an echo of *Macbeth*, for Lady Macbeth's mind runs over events in this way. But in her case the words are imbued with moral consciousness, which of course leads to her losing her mind.

Chapter 53

Rose and Harry Maylie are married. Oliver shares a small fortune with his half-brother, who later dies in prison abroad. Mr Brownlow adopts Oliver, Dr Losberne and Mr Grimwig become friends; while on the other side, so to speak, Noah becomes an informer, Mr and Mrs Bumble enter the workhouse as inmates, and Charley Bates goes straight. A memorial tablet to Agnes, Oliver's mother, is erected in the local church. All is rounded off – the good live happily on.

Commentary

There is little to add. The realism is over, the documentary is done, romantic and sentimental fiction requires a happy ending. This is what is provided, perhaps a timely reminder that we have been reading a story. Nevertheless, this sop to the reading public cannot detract from the high art with which most of that story is told.

asseveration i.e. 'I'll eat my head'.
grazier One who feeds cattle for market.

Revision questions on Chapters 41–53

1 Indicate the parts played by Rose Maylie and Mr Brownlow in unravelling the plot.

2 Give an account of the Artful Dodger's final scene in the novel.

3 What do you consider to be the most dramatic incident in these chapters?

4 Show how Dickens creates an atmosphere of dramatic tension in his focus on a) Nancy and b) Sikes's flight.

5 Describe Sikes's return to London and the consequences including the taking of Fagin.

6 In what ways do you consider the last chapter over-sentimental? Refer closely to the text.

Dickens's art in *Oliver Twist*
The characters

Dickens's characters are like no others. The ability to individualize abuses and eccentricities, the eye for the grotesque and, indeed, the ear for it, these are Dickens's main attributes.

His characters are unique because, though they may lack the full psychological integration of, say, Dorothea in *Middlemarch*, each has a full life of his own. It is not that they are 'round' or 'flat' by Forster's definition, but rather that they lead well-defined lives of their own within the fictional medium: they are not so much realistic as real. Thackeray diminished his own considerable achievements when he referred to himself as the 'puppet-master' in *Vanity Fair*, for Becky Sharp and her variegated companions live through the pages of that great novel without any pulling or manipulation, and we do not feel that they are packed away in a box at the end. They live on in their own independent lives, in our imagination, and the same is true of Dickens's characters. They are at once symbolic and real, for a novel is life writ large; they are not, for the most part, caricatures in the simple cartoon sense of that word, for their outlines shade into something of more human substance. In *Oliver Twist* the characters are generally black or white, but even here the greys are present: in Nancy and in Charley Bates, for example; and perhaps in the Dodger's befriending of Oliver (though we know that it is not entirely altruistic); and even in Sikes's frenzied redemptive rushes to and fro in the fire as he tries to shut out Nancy's eyes.

It must be allowed at the outset that the black or grey characters are the more convincing, and that Oliver, Rose Maylie and Dick, for instance, seem to inhabit a different area of the imagination — some would say an uncritical one — from that which houses Fagin, Sikes and the Dodger. For Dickens always had a fatal propensity to sentimental maudlin excess, which irks all but his most credulous readers — from Rose and Oliver here, through the irradiated Sissy Jupe of *Hard Times*, on to Lucy Manette in *A Tale of Two Cities*, thence to Riah, the old-clothes dealer-cum-Hebraic antidote to Fagin in *Our Mutual Friend*. But it is necessary to add that without those layers of sentiment there would be a loss to the reader, mainly because most of us do not read merely for academic or intellectual stimulus, but for emotional (in part sentimental) sustenance and expansion. And here Dickens is unsurpassed. Here that sweeping width of character delineation (undoubtedly the main reason for his enduring popularity) is seen in all the colourful, audible, idiosyncratic attractiveness, verve and ebullience of his nature. Dickens's social concerns are too well known to necessitate stressing here the expansive width of his attack during his writing life, but perhaps one should say that he was a man of strong feelings, and that sometimes those feelings (and this is another reason for his lasting popularity) were ambivalent in an unconscious sense.

The whole description of Fagin in the condemned cell is a calculated arraignment of evil in its ultimate degraded state; yet the humane chemistry of the writing is such that we are made to feel somehow the *waste*, the unloved, lopped life of an *old* man. We hate Fagin and we pity him, and perhaps subconsciously we are reminded of that celebrated evaluation of Milton's achievement in *Paradise Lost* that, so successfully and sympathetically had he presented Satan, he (Milton) was of the Devil's party without knowing it. Dickens is manifestly of God's party and asserts it, but sometimes his fallen characters successfully show his abiding concern for humanity, a concern that overshadows his inherent conservatism and over-sentimentalized Christian affiliations. Dickens detested the mob, hated and feared revolution, distrusted Trade Unionism and yet – and this is the paradox of the man and the artist – assailed with zeal and indignation some of the worst abuses in the establishment: the malpractices of the 'Circumlocution Office', the House of Commons (the national dust-heap) and the law.

Oliver

... a pale thin child, somewhat diminutive in stature, and decidedly small in circumference. But nature or inheritance had implanted a good sturdy spirit in Oliver's breast.

Oliver represents essential goodness – goodness of nature, not nurture – capable of resisting evil and triumphing over it. In terms of temptation Oliver has none; he is immune to the trials of human nature, lust for material gain or any corruption of the spirit or the flesh. He is the small boy, beaten, put down, humiliated but never degraded: for he has an inherent sense of right which causes him to defend his mother's name against the verbal abuse of a bigger boy (though he has never seen that mother); to resist stealing; to try to give the warning of the burglary at Chertsey; to spend innumerable hours gathering posies for Rose; to offer to pray with Fagin.

Such goodness is close to, but never feels the invitation of, martyrdom, whether it be at the hands of the workhouse master, the 'porochial' Board, Mr Fang, Sikes and Bulls-eye, the innocent servants at Chertsey, or Monks. The melodramatic strands of the plot, with some measure of Dickens's Gothic inheritance, enmesh Oliver. He cherishes the blessing of Dick and weeps to find that he is dead when he finally returns. He accepts Rose as a sister, then with delight as an aunt who will remain a sister. Earlier he has had the mystical communication with the portrait in Mr Brownlow's room; and always his sensitivity is tuned to consideration for others. He is intentionally drawn as 'green', affording much amusement to the Dodger and Charley Bates, but he has a certain sense of humour, a little surprising in one so pure, in that he enjoys the 'games' which the boys and the 'merry old gentleman' play. In fact the initial presentation of Fagin comes tellingly, cunningly, from Oliver's consciousness, the warmth of the den being the first real warmth the child has known. His name, chosen by Bumble, carries its own irony, for Oliver could not 'twist' anybody; he is merely born to be the victim of 'twisters'. But if realistically Oliver cannot ring true, symbolically he is essential in this fable of good besieged by evil.

Oliver Twist is an example, in a comparatively pure form, of the simple straightforward story, without the ramifications of sub-plots. The mystery of birth, the revelations of the inheritance, the questions of illegitimacy and adoption, all these bulk large in a plot that subserves the triumph of goodness. Oliver symbolizes the extreme – innocence; Charley Bates the middle – redemption (with Nancy); while the Dodger is a polar world away. It is an indication of Dickens's ambivalence and methods that we love – and perhaps secretly admire – the Dodger, whereas we are often indifferent (because he doesn't *live*) to Oliver. The cliché of evaluation, which is none the less true, is that in fiction the convincing portrayal of goodness and innocence is difficult, that of evil much easier.

Rose Maylie

'Oh! treat him kindly, Giles, for my sake!'

Rose is deservedly the aunt of Oliver, and Oliver deserves her. Two scenes condition our responses towards her; the first is when Harry Maylie proposes to her and is rejected by her unaccountable shame at her own position – her 'I'm not good enough for him' rationale. Rose is the first of a long line of Dickensian heroines who seem to owe much to Mary Hogarth, whose death during the writing of the novel occasioned Dickens such lifelong grief. These heroines are singularly saccharine and unsexual, with perhaps Esther Summerson (*Bleak House*), Amy Dorrit (*Little Dorrit*) and Lucy Manette (*A Tale of Two Cities*) representing the low watermark of insipidity. Mary Hogarth died, the source, one feels, of Rose's near-death; and the emotional re-working of Mary's death is a self-indulgence on the writer's part that enhances neither his plot nor his heroine. Roses's rejection of Harry Maylie is accompanied by the fulsome recourse to tears that is the standby of the 'wetter' Dickensian heroine:

There were tears in the eyes of the gentle girl, as these words were spoken; and when one fell upon the flower over which she bent, and glistened brightly in its cup, making it more beautiful, it seemed as though the outpouring of her fresh young heart, claimed kindred naturally, with the loveliest things in nature. (p.314)

One is forced to acknowledge, too, that the exchange with Nancy embraces the mawkish as well as the sentimental: Nancy is somewhat idealized, as the buried vein of goodness begins to yield its gold; but she and Rose do not speak the same language, breathe the same air or, even temporarily, communicate with anything approaching realism. Here is Rose responding in full flood, so to speak, to Nancy's avowal of loyalty to Sikes:

'Oh!' said the earnest girl, folding her hands as the tears coursed down her face, 'do not turn a deaf ear to the entreaties of one of your own sex, the first, I do believe, who ever appealed to you in the voice of pity and compassion.' (p.364)

These two quotations sufficiently indicate Rose's range; no glimmer of humour marks either her presentation or her reactions. She has the deadly seriousness of sentiment which makes her actions and her words consonant with the type of idealization common among Victorian writers: an appraisal of 'womanhood' that exalts the sweetly muted as the type for worship.

Harry Maylie

'I will lay at your feet, whatever of station or fortune I may possess; and if you still adhere to your present resolution, will not seek, by word or act, to change it.'

Harry flickers romantically into the action, once to propose, then to propose again, behaving in an avuncular (prophetically right) way to Oliver. He is given to the same extreme manner of avowal as Rose: as we will see in the section on *Style*, Dickens had a tendency towards the theatrical, evident here. And what better way of ending a scene on this level than by having Harry exit with commentary from the author, silence from himself! Yet his actions speak of that imminent and successful return before the final page:

She extended her hand again. But the young man caught her to his bosom; and imprinting one kiss on her beautiful forehead, hurried from the room. (p.318)

Fagin

... a very old shrivelled Jew, whose villainous looking and repulsive face was obscured by a quantity of matted red hair.

and Sikes

... a stoutly-built fellow of about five-and-thirty ... a broad heavy countenance with a beard of three days' growth and two scowling eyes;

These two share pride of place in the novel because of Dickens's remarkable ability to give his characters the actuality of *physical presence*. Sikes's abuse, whether it be of Bulls-eye or of Fagin or of Nancy, is frightening because we know that he is always on the edge of violence; here Dickens cleverly leads us on until the ultimate violence occurs and the enraged Sikes kills Nancy. But we cannot admit to the simplistic view of Sikes, for there is obviously more to him than the often repeated conventional appraisal of the brute housebreaker. Remember that Sikes does not leave Oliver until he has to, after the wounding at Chertsey; that he gets Oliver out of the house when the shot is fired; and remember too that he greatly appreciates Nancy's nursing of him after the escape. Consider also his tortured conscience after the killing; the constant fear of the eyes; his plunging into the fire to rescue others; and his abject return to the derelict house in Jacob's island, to be disowned by those of his kind. Even then his courage does not desert him, and he makes a bid for freedom against all odds. The student can investigate, more fully than space allows here, the quality of Sikes's characterization. Sikes is a recognizable study of a psychopath: a man given to violence but with a certain residual conscience; a villain, but with something more than villainy.

The same is not true of Fagin, who preaches number one but makes deadly sure that other numbers suffer, building up a network of evidence and intrigue destined to bring down all but himself. He is the corrupter of youth but, because of the ambivalence referred to earlier in Dickens's presentation, he is 'a merry old gentleman' in fact as well as in satirical intent, for he provides warmth and a home for those who would not otherwise have one. He is the Devil, yet an old man; he intrigues, yet feeds those who work for him. He is dishonest, devious, malign, grotesque, sullen, fearful, a manipulator intent on self-gain. He certainly believes in Wordsworth's dictum that the child is father of the man, though with something of a different emphasis to that intended by the poet. In short, he believes in catching them young and corrupting them for life. There is something terrifying in the presentation of Fagin, symbolizing as he does the extreme of the criminal life – that extreme from which there is no return, so that every action, even when reflex, is a criminal action; in fact, there is no aspect of the man that is not geared to turning deeds into capital. He has great pride in his inverted craft, and some of his last words are in praise of those who have worked for him: his delight in the Dodger's achievements is unbounded, even when he knows that the Artful is going to be transported.

Bumble and Mrs Bumble

A beadle ordered to hold his tongue! A moral revolution!

Mr Bumble, portly, pompous, a physical and moral coward, represents Dickens's central attack on the Poor Law system – the fact that those who administer it at the human level have little or no humanity to commend them. Bumble rests on his dignity, the ill-bred dignity of the man with an eye to the main chance. Once only, we get the impression that he is touched by something Oliver says; but he exists to implement the decisions of the Board, and the sound of his own voice and the taking of a 'little something' as befits his status are the two most important things in his life. There is nothing funnier in *Oliver Twist* than Bumble's courtship of Mrs Corney – his reckoning up of her portable assets is superb mime – and nothing more abject than his reduction by that lady two months after their marriage. Both represent a searching examination of hypocrisy and an exposure of it, and they underline a main Dickensian theme, the contrast between appearance and reality. To Mr Bumble, Mrs Corney appears the ideal, couldn't-say-boo-to-a-goose spouse; in fact, she is a tyrant. As soon as she becomes Mrs Bumble she reveals of what stern stuff she is made, and the assignation with Monks shows her quality. She is not afraid, whereas Bumble is in a visible state of funk. The implication is that the petty officers who deal with the poor are petty in mind, inconsiderate and intent on furthering their own ends. In a novel that sets out to establish the triumph of good over evil, they are fittingly reduced to being inmates of the workhouse they have abused.

Noah Claypole and Charlotte

. . . a large-headed, small-eyed youth

Noah represents another aspect of moral degeneracy: his treatment of Oliver shows the brutality of his nature; his taking advantage of Sowerberry his capacity for opportunism; his subordination of Charlotte his belief in the fact that it is a man's world. Paralleling the parish boy's progress, we have the charity boy's progress, for Noah rises in the world to become a police Informer, having betrayed Nancy, and of course Fagin, and having recourse later to various stratagems involving Charlotte and himself in implicating others. Two scenes involving Noah and Charlotte stand out: the first, when he is fed oysters and is caught kissing Charlotte by Bumble (Noah is something of a food and sex glutton) and the second, when he arrives at the Three Cripples, with Charlotte carrying the luggage, and is taken over by Fagin. He is a blubbering coward when anyone stands up to him, and we appreciate Charley Bates's laughter when Noah refers to him as a 'little boy'. Charlotte is merely a dupe, believing that the sun shines out of Noah, but we do not forget her attack on Oliver when Noah is crying.

Monks

... for he has desperate fits, and sometimes even bites his hands and covers them with wounds.

Monks is the stage villain of melodrama personified, with an added capacity for fits to give him an even more unlikely aura; he would be hissed when he appeared, but the reader's is more a silent hiss of the breath at his conception, evil without the personification and animation which vitalize both Fagin and Sikes.

The Dodger

He was, altogether, as roystering and swaggering a young gentleman as ever stood four feet six, or something less

The boy is already a man in terms of ability and a precocious knowledge of the seedy world: he has grown up before his language, so has to improvise with words just as he has to improvise at bookstalls and in thoroughfares in order to steal effectively and undetected. He is highly intelligent but deprived of home comforts and education; he is almost the prototype of the child today with the high IQ who becomes a delinquent. Always with an eye to the main chance, he turns his meeting with Oliver to advantage, spotting another trainee for Fagin. At the same time, he sees that Oliver eats and, in a sense, shows him more kindness than he has ever been shown in the past. He delights in picking Brownlow's pocket and having Oliver blamed, though he is worried about the joke when he realizes that Fagin will not see it in the same light. He has a certain vanity, as we see when Oliver cleans his 'trotter-cases', and always a degree of cunning; but we are forced to think of him as a little boy who has had to grow up too soon into a man's world. His bearing in the courtroom scene is remarkable, yet it is also pathetic. He will be transported, not for any of his great crimes, as Charley Bates bewails, but for a 'sneeze-box'. The Dodger cannot be put down, and threatens the magistrate with the 'Wice President' of the House of Commons; and he cannot be put out of our imaginations either. He exemplifies Dickens's characterization at its best, for there is no psychological preparation for the

Dodger. We do not see what made him as he is; he is superbly coined, but we are aware that at his back there stands a guilty society that has failed to channel his fine abilities, which have been transmuted into stealing and card-sharping.

Nancy

'She's a honour to her sex'

'The character of Nancy is the finest thing he ever did', said Dickens's great friend Wilkie Collins much later. The reader of *Oliver Twist* today will try to estimate if the girl's sudden spring of conscience grows out of character or out of artifice, whether the plot, which involves her seeking out Rose Maylie, drugging Sikes and being true to both sides, isn't a little too contrived. Dickens believed that it was not, and there is abundant testimony to his public readings of Sikes's murder of Nancy, which, so powerful was it, and so demanding on Dickens that it is thought it may have contributed to his premature death. But Dickens lived intensely through the creatures of his imagination, and he was always inclined to reserve for women a special, sentimental place. Nancy's loyalty to Sikes, who is her ponce, cannot be seen against a realistic context; it can be clearly seen, however, against the symbolic one, which is that evil can be reclaimed by the influence of good; and that in Oliver there exists the innocence that Nancy is conscious of having lost all those years ago to the insatiable Fagin. Nancy acts with courage, and her loyalty to Sikes is consistent; we remember his unsentimental response to her concern for the 'fine young chaps' who are executed; we remember her hysteria, her drinking, her secrecy, her care of Oliver by contrivance and her physical suffering at the hands of Sikes.

To return to the beginning of our account of Dickens's characterization: if Nancy is not realistic she is real, living in that rich world of the imagination that is Dickens's unique contribution to English fiction. That world defies further definition; for genius may take from life, but its salient quality is perhaps to give life itself.

Minor characters

With *Mrs Maylie* we face the awful limitations of perfection; she is a feminine Brownlow, in shadow, without the compensatory Grimwig. These early Dickensian 'goodies' give little promise of the later variants, which have degrees of goodness overlaid with other qualities (like the childlike simplicity of Mr Dick in *David Copperfield*, or the abrasive moodiness of Mr Jarndyce in *Bleak House*, which covers a multitude of kindnesses). Mrs Maylie adopts Rose, takes in the wounded Oliver, and speaks in an idiom of natural ease consonant with her breeding and position: 'my days are drawing to their close; and may mercy be shown to me as I show it to others. What can I do to save him, sir?' (p.269). The idea of a captive coterie of well-bred ladies and gentlemen waiting to adopt orphans who appear to be criminals is, of course, a far cry from the social realism and concern shown in other sections of the novel.

Admittedly *Mr Brownlow* has moments of life and eccentricity — and he has a function in the plot as the great unraveller of strands — but he is stereotyped, almost from the moment his pocket is picked by the Dodger. He is angry and alive enough to resent Fang and to hit back verbally; he is eccentric enough to sit determinedly on with the watch between himself and Grimwig. He is more than a match for Monks; compassionate towards Nancy; but beyond that he is good and good only, as we see when he finally adopts Oliver.

Mr Grimwig has all the potential, with his head-eating threat, of the later Dickensian eccentrics, with their extended imagery, language and gesture. (Mr Micawber's ability to ride the economic whirlwind; Uriah Heep's perpetual hand-washing, which cannot remove the inherent stain of character; Mr Merdle's constant taking of himself into custody — all these indicate the range Dickens was to achieve, and how the eccentric became the staple means of individualizing usage and abusage in character.) Mr Grimwig is never developed, for Dickens is concerned with plot, not sub-plot, with the text of Oliver's revelations, not the sub-text of psychological manifestation.

Dr Losberne admirably balances Grimwig in the novel (it is significant that they later become friends), and we see through him that Dickens already possesses that fine feeling for balance and unity, for contrast and order in characterization. The doctor brings a genuine breath of life into the claustrophobic goodness of the house at Chertsey, with its melodrama-cum-comedy duo of Brittles and Giles on the one hand and the arrival of Blathers and Duff on the other. *Oliver Twist* is a sombre novel and it is sometimes hard to remember and accept that parts of it were being written before *Pickwick Papers* was finished; yet comedy elements like those mentioned above are balanced in the structure by the comedy of the boys in Fagin's den.

Blathers and Duff, who suffer the edge of Dickens's satirical intent, not only 'balance' the servants in this part of the plot, but *Fang* in the other. These police officers are, of course, incompetent, and the implication is that their incompetence, the fact that they are easily hoodwinked by the Losberne manoeuvre, that each has his own beliefs, suspicions, anecdotes, hypotheses – all irrelevant to the case in hand – all serve to underline the serious deficiencies of the force. This is yet another Dickensian barb at the law.

Brittles and Giles represent, at one level, a kindly satire upon 'brave' old retainers and on the perfectly natural capacity we have to distort and lie a little in the interests of enhanced status. Brittles, as the echo to the somewhat pompous assertions of Giles, makes the pair a music-hall comedy act, just indeed as are Blathers and Duff. But Brittles and Giles have behind them the comparative innocence of kitchen servants' long service, where loss of face or maintenance of reputation, light verbal bullying and tired sycophantic responses are the order of the day.

Chertsey is a curious episode in *Oliver Twist*. Once again we find Oliver in a strange house which is really a home to him, with an aura of goodness surrounding him just as there was in Brownlow's house, with Mrs Bedwin nursing him and refusing thereafter to hear any evil of him. If we penetrate below their comic function, we find that Brittles and Giles are possessed of the same quality of humanity as those above stairs. Although Giles fires the pistol that wounds Oliver, and although his reactions are boastful in a benign way, he is very relieved to know that he has not wounded Oliver seriously. He is a simple soul, exercising a kindly patronage among his fellow servants. Brittles is, of course, the perpetual boy of the household, his status and responses determined by the junior position he will always hold.

Mrs Bedwin approximates to Mrs Maylie, but she of course is a housekeeper, while Mrs Maylie is a lady; nevertheless, the upstairs-downstairs humanity of the two houses is a further strand of unity in the structure of the novel. Mrs Bedwin is kindness and trust personified, always believing in Oliver's innocence. She is a 'motherly old lady, very neatly and precisely dressed ', and she weeps with pretty fair regularity.

Of little *Dick* not a great deal can be said; he knows of his own doom, wishes to join his little sister in heaven, and utters the first blessing that Oliver has heard. He symbolizes the maltreatment and death of the many, the what-might-have-been for Oliver. He has little fictional – and even less real – life.

Sowerberry is a caricature, well-disposed towards Oliver as long as he can use him, but kept under the matrimonial thumb, so that he is forced to beat Oliver for the assault on Noah. He uses him advantageously as a mute, and always has an eye to business. *Mr Gamfield*, too, is a caricature; his horse-beating and his deal with the Board indicate his brutality. And the *gentleman in the white waistcoat*, who is always saying that Oliver was born to be hanged, is another of the 'humane' members of the Board anxious to get rid of Oliver.

Mrs Mann, the matron of the branch workhouse, is another emphatic short portrayal of hypocrisy, her entertainment of Bumble being a masterpiece of pretended care for the children. *Amy, Martha* and old *Sally* hardly register except as hags reduced to haggery by the workhouse system regardless of what they were outside, and *Agnes Fleming* dies too soon (after all, Oliver is illegitimate!) to be idealized in the flesh.

But it is when we move into Fagin's den or, before that, when Oliver meets the Dodger on the way to London, that the life of the novel emerges through a series of characters, strongly individualized, who represent the criminal elements in all their ingenuity and degradation. The Dodger's apprentice friend, *Charley Bates*, is almost as successfully if not as colourfully drawn; he is frequently seized with laughter, either at the contemplation of Oliver's innocent face or, when he is re-taken, his 'heavy swell' clothes. He lacks the Dodger's brilliance, either of vocabulary or ability in the professional sense, but he shows a moral growth somewhat akin to Nancy's – one has to question the truth of it. Charley is convincing *until* he attacks Sikes; he certainly is not lacking in courage, as this assault proves, and later he reforms and becomes a grazier.

Tom Chitling is essentially gullible and 'fancies' Bet, which makes him a bigger butt than usual so far as the others are concerned; while *Flash Toby Crackit* reveals himself to be something of a coward after the robbery, though he is always eloquent, and as sharp as the Dodger in terms of cards and language – though Toby's is the conventional thieves' slang of the time. He is a ladies' man with, alas, little chance to show it during the action of the novel. *Barney*, the adenoidal young Jew at the Three Cripples, is certainly a villainous character, *bud he dod do but* in the story except to help in the planning of the robbery and to put Fagin in the way of dealing with Nancy and taking over Noah Claypole.

Style

To say that Dickens's style is richly varied is in a sense to be guilty of a truism yet, such is its richness and individuality, one is forced to acknowledge the quality of its range. In this section the main stylistic devices employed by Dickens in *Oliver Twist* are outlined. Some of them are highly sophisticated and perhaps merit sophisticated definition; others are typical of the natural verve and flow of an ebullient personality. Dickens had trained himself as a journalist and was quite capable of using journalistic tricks of the trade: emotive power, rhetorical invocation or propagandist innuendo. It is part of his unique talent that he could touch the heights of poetry as well. In his prose we find the coexistence of the maudlin and the searching, the commonplace and the exotic, the oratorical and the simple; so that the reader is excited and stimulated into response – whether aesthetic or emotional or both.

In a telling article entitled 'George Eliot and the Omniscient Author Convention', W.J. Harvey convincingly demonstrates the modes of author-control exercised by that great novelist: we should need a book (and there probably is one) to do justice to the overt and subtle manifestations of Dickens's personal voice in his own works. For there is no mistaking the fact that the voice we listen to most in *Oliver Twist* is that of Dickens himself. Generally it is ironic and compassionate, almost as if in deliberate contrast to the voices of Bumble, Fagin, Sikes, or even Monks. On the first page of the novel we find just such a usage: the author's 'I' is in abeyance later, but here it is used to establish a relationship with the reader: a conversational, mutual exploration of the state of the workhouse – 'I will assign no fictitious name ... Although I am not disposed to maintain' (p.45).

The effect is one of intimacy: this is not the lecture of a literary gentleman, but the confidence of a concerned human being. Having established the tone Dickens extends it, telling the reader by the end of Chapter 2, 'As I purpose to show in the sequel whether the white-waistcoated gentleman was right or not' (p.58). With this achieved, Dickens can let the narrative take over, but occasionally he employs his own voice in ironic contrast to the reality he is describing. Thus Chapter 4 opens, 'In great families, when an advantageous place cannot be obtained, either in possession . . . for the young man who is growing up, it is a very general custom to send him to sea' (p.68). Now Oliver is of the 'great family' of the poor, so in fact he has no inheritance anyway; and, when the Board decides that Oliver should go to sea, Dickens is attacking in his own voice the shuffling-off of social responsibility. Yet in the same chapter the author's tone with regard to those who fashion 'humane' laws is unequivocally savage:

I wish some well-fed philosopher, whose meat and drink turn to gall within him; whose blood is ice, whose heart is iron; could have seen Oliver Twist clutching at the dainty viands that the dog had neglected. (p.74)

Compare this quotation with the previous one, and you will see what is meant by Dickens's range. This is blunt irony, but it underlines Dickens's ability to assume a role. At one stage in the novel he refers to Mr Grimwig's ventriloquial capacity, and perhaps here it would be fitting to note his own: he speaks with many voices, but they are all imbued with the tone of common humanity. Again, the alert student will search out other statements in the author's own voice, and see what they contribute to the themes and concerns of *Oliver Twist*.

Pride of place is given to Dickens's voice, for his use of it leads happily to a related effect, the superb control of the *ironic* aside or qualification that so enriches our contemplation of character. Sometimes these fertile extensions of an idea are redolent of his comic spirit: thus Mr Fang, administering the law, is described in terms appropriate to his calling in 'he might have brought an action against his countenance for libel, and have recovered heavy damages' (p.120). A slightly different form is apparent when Mr Bumble says to his 'fascinator', 'What a opportunity for a joining of hearts and housekeepings!' (p.249), or there is the simple irony of Mrs Sowerberry's blaming herself for Oliver's 'revolt' when she observes 'this comes of being liberal!' (p.93). There is, further, the mimic irony of Mr Bumble's actions:

He opened the closet, counted the teaspoons, weighed the sugar-tongs, closely inspected a silver milk-pot to ascertain that it was of the genuine metal, and, having satisfied his curiosity on these points, put on his cocked hat corner-wise, and danced with much gravity four distinct times round the table. (p.223)

Dickens's ironic modes run throughout *Oliver Twist* and are a constant source of delight to the reader, mainly because they are unpredictable, part of the inwardly varied nature of his treatment of his subjects. Closely related to the ironic manner is the satirical, and in *Oliver Twist* this is frequently seen in the theatrical associations, which are indicated in the textual notes. The satire directed against Mr Fang is barbed, for the courtroom is a stage on which he gives his daily one-man show; not so, however, in the case of Blathers and Duff who are, so to speak, a permanent repertory company of incompetence – though their cross-talk act is sufficiently entertaining in itself. But they always need an audience, and their interrogation of Brittles and Giles and the conclusions they come to are Dickens's satirical attack on the dull-witted, unimaginative routine-mongers of the force. Nancy's affectation at finding her 'little brother' is hardly satire, but it is a further use of the theatrical *motif* that runs through the text. For Nancy to reclaim Oliver she has to appear what she is not; for Oliver to be thought a criminal he must appear what *he* is not – a thief. To Oliver the boys appear to be playing a game – in reality they are in strict training; Mrs Corney appears pliable to Bumble but he finds to his cost that she is obdurate, inflexible.

Dickens achieves all this through a superb stylistic effect, that of describing what is *seen* and only revealing later what is not seen. Fagin appears to be 'a merry old gentleman' (notice how Dickens shows Oliver's reaction) but he is a rogue. Mr Grimwig appears irascible, but he is kind. One could go on exploring this aspect, but it would be as well to curb the tendency now, for there is the other side of the coin, the reality that is genuine, namely the fact of Sikes and the melodramatic fact of Monks. Dickens is using *contrast* here, and indeed the novel is structured on just that balance between the real and the unreal, between, if you like, Sikes and Rose Maylie.

Another aspect of Dickens's style is his command of the *grotesque*, seen in physical description (Fagin and Bumble); the grotesque in speech (the Dodger and Barney); and the grotesque in appetite (Noah Claypole). The Cruikshank illustrations to the text reflect the essentially *visual* grotesqueness of Dickens's work: Oliver asking for more, or Fagin in the condemned cell, typify this quality. Barney's nasal pronunciation and the Dodger's raids on the undigested articulate – look at the courtroom scene again – show Dickens's supreme awareness of the idiosyncratic that has its origin in physical or social malformation.

The *dialogue* throughout *Oliver Twist* is superb, and the most vivid aspect of it is the thieves' slang or the colloquial usage of the boys as distinct from the received standard of Rose Maylie, Mr Brownlow and the essentially middle-class group who stand in contrast to them. Here is Toby Crackit studying Oliver: 'Wot an inwalable boy that'll make, for the old ladies' pockets in chapels! His mug is a fortun' to him' (p.209); here is Monks: 'Curses light upon your head, and black death upon your heart, you imp! (p.298); and here is Sikes in desperation, talking to himself:

'A good hiding-place, too. They'll never expect to nab me there, after this country scent. Why can't I lie by for a week or so, and, forcing blunt from Fagin, get abroad to France? Damme, I'll risk it.' (p.430)

Again, there is a range in the control of the spoken word, but the language of Toby Crackit and of Sikes has the ring of truth, that of Monks the hiss of melodrama. Occasionally, the language of *sentiment* predominates, as indeed it does in that whole section devoted to Oliver's country stay with the Maylies. Here is a typical description:

Then, he had his own lesson for the next day to prepare; and at this, he would work hard, in a little room which looked into the garden, till evening came slowly on, when the ladies would walk out again, and he with them: listening with such pleasure to all they said: and so happy if they wanted a flower that he could climb to reach, or had forgotten anything he could run to fetch: that he could never be quick enough about it. (p.291)

Sentimental effusions like this – notice the regularity of the language, which has none of the urgent and unpredictable rhythms of life to animate it – do not occur merely in descriptions; they are implicit in dialogue, so that Rose speaks flowers, breathes pure scent from this incorruptible landscape, and her tears are, of course, dew. It is this uncritical strain in Dickens that makes for the unevenness of *Oliver Twist*, and indeed of much of his work.

Compare the above with this description of Fagin's other den, where Oliver is taken and which he is free to examine after some time:

In all the rooms, the mouldering shutters were fast closed: the bars which held them were screwed tight into the wood; the only light which was admitted, stealing its way through round holes at the top: which made the rooms more gloomy, and filled them with strange shadows. (p.179)

Here the house is *symbolic* of criminality, its lack of light, its bars (prison-like), its 'mouldering shutters' (physical decay equivalent to moral corruption). This is fine writing of a particularly sombre type, but it looks forward to the superb symbolism of Mrs Clennam's decaying house in *Little Dorrit*, or the description of the Marshalsea in that same novel, the prison from which her father never escapes – even when he is far beyond its confines at the rich dinner where he dies.

Oliver Twist is lush in the casual imagery of a fertile imagination, so that Dickens often writes metaphorically, or provides a comparison from the rich storehouse of his observation ('as if he had lived inside the ball of St. Paul's Cathedral'), while a row of elm boards look to Oliver 'like high-shouldered ghosts with their hands in their breeches-pockets'. Running throughout are images of death and the grave and the worm, all underpinning the main theme of decay and corruption, while in the latter parts of the novel the imagery that surrounds Fagin is animalistic in import – Fagin is in his 'lair' and he has a few 'fangs' like those of a dog or rat, or he appears to be searching for 'offal'. The moral tone of such images is very strong indeed.

But perhaps Dickens's supreme achievement in *Oliver Twist* is that ability to create atmosphere and to sustain *graphic narrative* with all the force of immediacy. Two instances, both occurring late in the novel, are the flight of Sikes, and Fagin in the condemned cell. Both deal with imprisonment, the one of the mind and the other of the physical being. Sikes can never escape his deed, but his efforts to do so are written with a sustained and sympathetic identification on the part of the author. (In nineteenth-century fiction, perhaps only Hetty's journey in despair in *Adam Bede* or Tess's trek to Flintcomb Ash in *Tess of the D'Urbervilles* bear any comparison, but for obvious reasons they lack the *frenzy* of Sikes's mood). The physical doubling-back is the mental equivalent of undoing what one has done: there is no escape, nor would there have been if Sikes had made the leap. And Fagin, too, is trapped within himself, reverting to the past in the anguish of trying to escape the present. Two other aspects enter here: Dickens, who feared the mob, conveys with a deadly atmospheric power the storming of the house where Sikes is hiding, and (he was to repeat this again later) the silent courtroom mob, which gives voice only when Fagin is sentenced to death.

General questions

1 Show how Dickens creates atmosphere in any *three* incidents. You should pay particular attention to the language used.

Note-form guidelines

(a) *Introduction* – Dickens the master of atmosphere of various kinds – give instances – then select three which indicate variety.

(b) Two paragraphs on atmosphere of *fear* – either Fagin in the death cell or in court, or Sikes's flight. Example – Sikes's flight – emphasis on light and the fact that Sikes can't face it – use of repetition to show workings of his mind – detail (hair on end of club) – retracing steps – inside mind all the time – Hatfield incident with stains – working out guilt and fear in rescuing others from fire – return to London – attempt to dispose of dog before he does so.

(c) Atmosphere of *humour* – Bumble's courtship of Mrs Corney. Detail from Chapters 23 and 27 – the cup of tea – the moving of the chair round the table – the kiss – the interruption – Mr Bumble's inspection of Mrs Corney's china etc. – the return of Mrs Corney – 'Peppermint' – more discussion of mutual economics. Bring out the humour – grotesque etc.

(d) Atmosphere of *sentiment* – Chapters 32 and 33 in particular – Oliver and nature – his walks – talks – service to Rose – three months (give selective detail) – illness of Rose – build-up of time – Losberne's reassurance – Harry Maylie – proposal to Rose (extend beyond these chapters for this).

(e) *Conclusion* – Dickens's ability illustrated by the above – contrast vivid imaginative and realistic effects with mawkish and sentimental ones.

2 Write a critical account of the workhouse/farm system in *Oliver Twist*, indicating clearly the main areas of Dickens's attack.

3 What do you find (a) pathetic and (b) comic in the first few chapters of the novel? You should refer closely to the text in your answer.

4 Write a character study of Mr Bumble and show how he influences the main plot of the novel.

5 Write an essay on why you feel/do not feel sympathetic towards Oliver.

6 Compare and contrast Oliver's early experiences in the workhouse and with Sowerberry, with his early experiences in Fagin's den.

7 By a close study of selected incidents, write a character sketch of Bill Sikes. Is he as bad as he at first appears?

8 Write an account of Dickens's use of his own voice in the novel, using examples other than those which appear in this study aid.

9 Writing of Nancy, Dickens observed of her character that 'It is true'. How far would you agree or disagree with this statement.

10 Write a detailed account of the part played in *Oliver Twist* by (a) The Artful Dodger and (b) Charley Bates.

11 Who do you find the most convincing of the 'good' characters and why? Refer closely to incidents in the novel in support of your views.

12 'His concern is always human injustice.' What aspects of injustice is Dickens mainly concerned with in *Oliver Twist*?

13 What, for you, are the most *realistic* incidents in the novel? Give reasons for your answer.

14 Write an account of the part played in the action by any of the following: (a) Blathers and Duff; (b) Giles and Brittles; (c) Mrs Maylie and Mr Grimwig; (d) Noah Claypole and Charlotte.

15 Describe the part played in the novel by Monks and Mr Brownlow. Which of the two do you find the more convincing character?

16 Describe the style employed by Dickens in any two sections of the novel, bringing out clearly the effectiveness of the usage.

17 Who do you find the most interesting character in the novel, and why?

18 From Dickens's account, what do you learn of the criminal underworld of the time?

19 In what ways does Dickens's *irony* reinforce his moral attitude? You should quote from the text in support of your views.

20 Write an account of Fagin and his activities. Do you feel any pity for him? Or none?

21 Who seems to you to be the most fully drawn of all the characters in *Oliver Twist*? Once again, quote in support of your views.

22 Write an essay on Dickens's use of the *grotesque* in *Oliver Twist*.

23 Compare and contrast the Dodger's courtroom appearance with that of Oliver before Mr Fang.

24 Write an essay on the *appearance/reality* theme and say what effect it has on our appraisal of any two or three of the characters.

25 Write an essay on the structure of *Oliver Twist*, showing how Dickens makes effective use of parallel and contrast in the novel.

26 'Ruined by sentimental excess'. How far is this true of *Oliver Twist*?

27 By some examination of the plot and action of *Oliver Twist*, account for its continued popularity.

28 Write an essay on the most *exciting* sequence in *Oliver Twist*. How does Dickens maintain the narrative tension?

29 What aspects of human nature does Dickens most despise? You may refer to three or four characters in your answer.

30 'Dominated by the figure of Fagin – the Devil'. How far would you agree with this estimate of *Oliver Twist*?

Further reading

Charles Dickens: A Critical Introduction K.J. Fielding (Longman)
The Dickens Theatre Robert Garis (Oxford University Press)
The Moral Art of Dickens Barbara Hardy (Athlone Press)
Who's Who in Dickens John Greaves (Elm Tree Books)
The Dickens Encyclopaedia ed. Arthur Hayward (Routledge)
Dickens and Women Michael Slater (Dent)
Dickens and Charity Norris Pope (Macmillan)
Dickens and the Invisible World Harry Stone (Macmillan)

The above is merely a selection from the mass, but the first book provides a most sensible and balanced introduction to Dickens. For the student who is completely won over to him there is the opportunity to join the Dickens Fellowship and receive copies of *The Dickensian*, a magazine devoted to the writer.